Experimental Ichthyology

Experimental Ichthyology

SK Garg
Professor Fisheries, Department of Zoology and Aquaculture
CCS Haryana Agricultural University, Hisar

Anita Bhatnagar
Department of Zoology and Aquaculture
CCS Haryana Agricultural University, Hisar

Alok Kalla
Department of Zoology and Aquaculture
CCS Haryana Agricultural University, Hisar

MS Johal
Professor, Department of Zoology
Punjab University, Chandigarh

CBS

CBS Publishers & Distributors Pvt Ltd

New Delhi • Bengaluru • Chennai • Kochi • Kolkata • Mumbai
Hyderabad • Jharkhand • Nagpur • Patna • Pune • Uttarakhand

Experimental Ichthyology

ISBN: 978-81-239-0771-0

First Edition: 2002
Reprint: 2021

Published by **Satish Kumar Jain** and produced by **Varun Jain** for

CBS Publishers & Distributors Pvt Ltd
4819/XI Prahlad Street, 24 Ansari Road, Daryaganj, New Delhi 110 002, India.
Ph: 011-23289259, 23266861, 23266867 Website: www.cbspd.com
Fax: 011-23243014 e-mail: delhi@cbspd.com; cbspubs@airtelmail.in.

Corporate Office: 204 FIE, Industrial Area, Patparganj, Delhi 110 092
Ph: 011-4934 4934 Fax: 011-4934 4935
e-mail: publishing@cbspd.com; publicity@cbspd.com

Branches

- **Bengaluru:** Seema House 2975, 17th Cross, K.R. Road, Banasankari 2nd Stage, Bengaluru 560 070, Karnataka, India
  Ph: +91-80-26771678/79 Fax: +91-80-26771680 e-mail: bangalore@cbspd.com
- **Chennai:** 7, Subbaraya Street, Shenoy Nagar, Chennai 600 030, Tamil Nadu, India
  Ph: +91-44-26680620, 26681266 Fax: +91-44-42032115 e-mail: chennai@cbspd.com
- **Kochi:** 42/1325, 1326, Power House Road, Opp KSEB, Ernakulum, Kochi 682 018, Kerala, India
  Ph: +91-484-4059061-65,67 Fax: +91-484-4059065 e-mail: kochi@cbspd.com
- **Kolkata:** 6/B, Ground Floor, Rameswar Shaw Road, Kolkata-700014 (West Bengal), India
  Ph: +91-33-2289-1126, 2289-1127, 2289-1128 e-mail: kolkata@cbspd.com
- **Mumbai:** PWD Shed, Gala no 25/26, Ramchandra Bhatt Marg, Next to JJ Hospital Gate no. 2, Opp. Union Bank of India, Noorbaug Mumbai-400009, Maharashtra, India
  Ph: +91-22-66661880/89 e-mail: mumbai@cbspd.com

Representatives

• Hyderabad	0-9885175004	• Jharkhand	0-9811541605	• Nagpur	0-9421945513
• Patna	0-9334159340	• Pune	0-9623451994	• Uttarakhand	0-9716462459

Printed at Glorious Printers, Jhilmil Industrial Area, Delhi, India

Preface

Literature dealing with the practicals in Ichthyology is scant and also scattered. In this book an attempt has been made to bring together the diverse facets of practical exercises on various aspects of fisheries in a consolidated form, to induct students and researchers into scientific investigations.

The book has been divided into eight chapters. Chapter 1 deals with the experiments on physico-chemical and biological characteristics of water and sediment. Chapter 2 deals with the pond management practices and 3 with fishing gears. Chapter 4 is devoted to experiments on fish nutrition. Management of fish health and hygiene are discussed in Chapter 5, whereas Chapter 6 deals with fish physiology and behaviour. In Chapter 7, experiments on fish reproduction and breeding have been described. Chapter 8 covers the methodology on age and growth studies including population dynamics. Key for the identification of common fishes and morphometric measurements are given in Chapter 9. For better understanding of the subject, solved and unsolved exercises have also been included in each chapter.

Experiments have been written in a manner that it will reduce the time required for instruction at the beginning of each exercise and thus to make more time available for the actual experiment. In general, each experiment consists of a brief introduction to the topic and the principle involved therein to help the readers to draw precise and concise conclusion, followed by materials required, procedures and methods of recording the observations. Most of the basic methods suggested herein are according to the standard procedures, however, some have been modified in order to make them more understandable. We have tried to compile all the relevant information at one place. Thus, the book is intended for wide audience. It is our belief that the book shall prove to be useful to the students, teachers and researchers alike pursuing their activities in understanding the various aspects of fisheries. Valuable suggestions, comments for improvement and addition in subsequent editions will be welcome.

Hisar, 2001

S.K. Garg
Anita Bhatnagar
Alok Kalla
M.S. Johal

Acknowledgements

To accomplish such a big task, it would have been insurmountable without the help and criticism from various quarters. We also wish to gratefully acknowledge the material provided for the book by various colleagues and friends.

Our thanks go to Shri B.S. Saharan, Director and Dr. S.C. Agarwal, Joint Director, Fisheries Department, Government of Haryana, Dr. K.L. Jain, Head Deptt. of Zoology and Aquaculture Professor (Dr.) V.P. Sabhlok, Deptt. of Zoology and Aquaculture; Dr. C.L. Goswami, Department of Botany and Plant Physiology, CCS HAU, Hisar for multifarious help and encouragement and for their useful comments and advice on the manuscript.

We are highly indebted to Dr. Randhir Singh, Professor of Biochemistry, formerly Dean and Coordinator Research, CCS Haryana Agricultural University, Hisar for his guidance, inspiration and encouragement during the course of collection of materials for this book. We offer our sincere thanks to Neeru Narula for help in reading the manuscript at various stages, to Sh. Rajpal Dhankhar for computer typing the draft and to Mr. Kuljit Mann for drawing the figures.

Authors

Contents

LIST OF EXERCISES

Chapter 1

1. Calculate species diversity from the given data by Marglef's diversity index and compare it with Shanon and Weaver's diversity index.
2. Diurnal changes in DO concentrations are given. Calculate net primary productivity
3. Collect water samples, identify and prepare whole mounts of both phytoplankton and zooplankton.

Chapter 2

1. Calculate the quantity of piscicides required for treatment of a pond/water body.
2. Calculate the quantity of earth required for making bundh of a given pond.
3. Find out the number of fish seed to be transported in a given volume of water.
4. Ask students to write a field report of their visit to the fish farm.

Chapter 3

1. You are being provided a freshly used cotton/hemp/synthetic net. How you will proceed for its proper maintenance ?
2. Draw diagrams of important crafts and gears used for fishing in your area.

Chapter 4

1. Calculate the following parameters from the given data :
   (i) Growth (% gain in body weight)
   (ii) Growth per day in percentage body weight
   (iii) Digestibility or food absorption efficiency (%)
   (iv) Food consumption per day in per cent body weight
   (v) Feed conversion ratio (FCR)
   (vi) Gross conversion efficiency (GCE)
   (vii) Protein efficiency ratio (PER)
2. Calculate the following parameters : (a) growth (b) growth rate (c) arithmetic mean body weight (d) specific growth rate

Chapter 5

1. Collect and identify fish parasites and draw diagrams
2. Identify the disease/s from the infected fish specimen

Chapter 6

1. Compare the melanophore index of pinealectomised fish with those of normal fish.
2. Compare the melanophore indices of dark background adapted and light background adapted fish.
3. Study the effect of melatonin and epinephrine on melanophore index and compare your results with fish injected with saline solution
4. Study the effect of salinity, temperature and epinephrine on rate of respiration and oxygen consumption

Chapter 7

1. Take out the gonads (male and female organs) from a catfish/carp during the different phases of reproductive cycle. Draw labelled diagrams and also plot GSI.
2. Fix the gonads (ovaries/testes), prepare histological slides and identify various stages.

Chapter 8

1. Collect scales from different fish species and use for determining the age of the species.
2. On the basis of the given length size data draw histograms of appropriate size groups and give suitable interpretation of the data.
3. Plot a graph between anterior scale radius and mean total length of a fish from the given data.
4. What is CF and explain the following formula:

   L' = S'/S (L-CF)+CF
5. Compute the standard length for the following data where (a) the scale marginal radius at the time of capture was 120 mm, (b) standard length—250 mm, (c) anterior scale radius measurements 30.0, 70.0, 90.0, 100.0, 110.0 mm.
6. Calculate length-weight relationship from the given data for given fish population.
7. If total population = 1000, unmarked population = 900, marked population = 100, calculate population of fish and per cent error.

Chapter 9

1. Collect the common fish fauna from ponds/tanks and canals, identify, classify and write characters

CHAPTER 1

Water and Sediment Analysis

Collection and Preservation of Water Samples

Collect water samples from the desired depth preferably in polythene bottles. It is important to start analysis as soon as possible. Store the samples in a proper way as follows :

Sample storage methods

Parameter to be determined	Preservation	Shelf life
Dissolved oxygen	Fix the samples immediately	24 hours
Free CO_2	-	Determine immediately
Acidity-Alkalinity	Refrigeration at 4°C	24 hours
BOD	Refrigeration at 4°C	6 hours
COD	Refrigeration at 4°C	7 days
Chlorides	Refrigeration not necessary	7 days
Hardness	Refrigeration not required	7 days
NH_4-N	0.8 ml $H_2 SO_4$/L- and store at 4°C	7 days
Nitrogen Kjeldahl	" "	7 days
Nitrogen, nitrate- nitrite	" "	7 days
Orthophosphate	40 mg $HgCl_2$ l^{-1} 4°C	7 days
Conductivity	4°C	7 days
Total solids	4°C	7 days
pH	-	Determine immediately
Turbidity	Store in dark	7 days

Experiment 1.1 : *How samples are collected from shallow ponds ? Write notes on the following :*

(a) *Dussart water sampler*

(b) *Ruttner water sampler*

Water samplers are not used in shallow water bodies. To collect a water sample from a shallow pond, rinse a bucket with pond water and fill it with samples collected from various sites and depths. Mix well. Store the samples in rinsed polyethylene/ glass bottles and close them tightly.

The following types of water samplers are employed to collect the water samples from deeper water bodies.

(a) ***Dussart water sampler*** **:** This sampler works on the principle of displacement of air and consists of a bottle with a weight at the bottom and a graduated rope tied to its neck. The opening of the flask has two holes for fitting two glass tubes, one short and the other long. The outer end of these tubes are interconnected by a flexible rubber tube tied to the rope in such a way that it can be pulled out by a slight jerk to the rope. For collection of water sample it is lowered in water to the desired depth and then the tube is pulled out by a jerk on the rope, which opens glass tubes. Water rushes into the bottle through the longer tube displacing air out through the short one. As soon as the flask is completely filled, the sampler is taken out of the water body (Fig. 1.1).

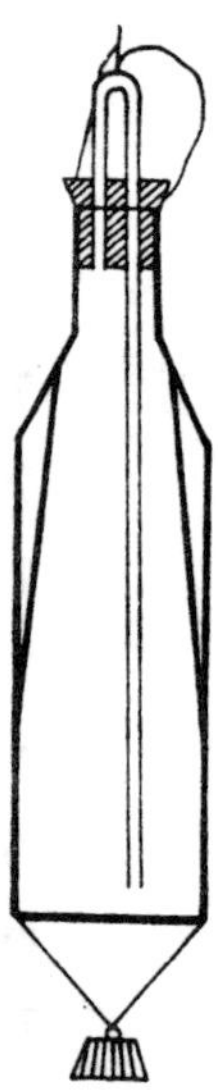

Fig. 1.1. **Dussart water sampler.**

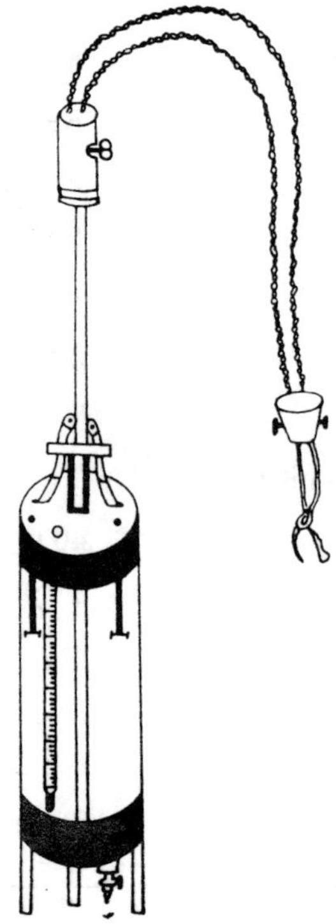

Fig. 1.2. **Ruttner water sampler.**

(b) ***Ruttner water sampler*** : It is made up of a glass cylinder with upper and lower lids. The lids remain open due to a trap mechanism and can be closed by a messenger as and when desired. For sample collection the sampler is lowered in water in open condition upto the desired depth and is then closed by sending the messenger through the graduated rope. The weight hits and opens the trap mechanism causing the closer of the upper and lower lids. The sampler is then taken out of the water, and the water sample is then collected from the tap at the lower lid (Fig. 1.2).

Physico-chemical characteristics of water

Experiment 1.2 : *Determination of water temperature.*

It is a very important factor for the pond productivity.

Materials

Precision Thermometer, 0-50°C or any electronic temperature meter with a probe.

Both centigrade (Celsius) or Farenheit thermometers can be employed for recording the water temperature.

Conversion : To find degree °C, substract 32 from degree °F and divide by 1.8.

To find degree °F, multiply degrees °C by 1.8 and add 32 or use the following formula for conversion :

$$\frac{C}{5} = \frac{F-32}{9}$$

Experiment 1.3 : *Determination of transparency.*

Transparency is the measure of range of light penetration. The depth to which light attenuation reaches 1% of the surface value is taken as compensation depth and indicates the lower limit of trophogenic zone. It is inversely proportional to turbidity of water which in turn is directly proportional to the amount of suspended organic and inorganic matter present in the water.

Materials

Secchi Disc and a tape with measurement marks.

Secchi Disc is a metallic disc with black and white markings (Fig. 1.3).

Principle

By lowering a black and white painted disk into the water one can roughly measure the depth to which one can see into the water. This is a very simple method to compare the visibility depth of different waters.

Procedure

Slowly lower the disk into the water until it just disappears- note this depth -A.

Lower the disk somewhat further, then slowly raise it until it reappears-note the depth-B.

The average value of these two readings is taken for the final secchi disk visibility

$$\frac{A+B.}{2}$$

Note: The observed depth is dependent on weather conditions and also on the observer. It is better if one observer records all readings and establishes a standard set of operating conditions for himself.

In these days turbidity meters of various makes are also available, which are easy to operate, therefore, transparency can also be measured directly as turbidity in NTU (Nephelo turbidity units). The values of transparency are inversely proportional to turbidity.

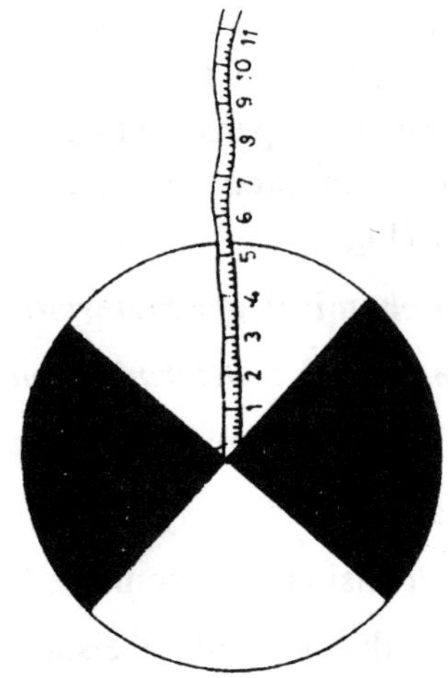

Fig. 1.3. Secchi disc.

Experiment 1.4 : Determination of water flow/water velocity.

A water body with all its components both (biotic and abiotic, are in motion due to wind action, incoming water, outflowing water and silt etc. The water current affects the transfer of materials and heat in a system. There are several methods to measure the rate of water flow :

(a) Surface float method

Materials

(i) Bamboo poles

(ii) Stop watch

(iii) Floats

(iv) Measuring tape

Procedure

- Fix two poles keeping a known distance (say 10-20 meters) along the direction of flow.
- Throw the float (a piece of wood or lastic etc.) and note the direction and time taken by the float to cover the dist ace between the two poles.
- Use a stop watch for recording time.

Calculations

$$V = \frac{d}{1.2t}$$

Where,

V = is the velocity of water in mS^{-1} (meters per second) d = distance travelled by the float

t = time in seconds

1.2 = is the factor which accounts for the fact that surface velocities are normally about 1.2 times higher

(b) Flow meter method

Flow meters are available in the market which gives accurate velocity in meters per second and are generally used in fast moving larger water bodies such as rivers and stream etc.

Experiment 1.5 **:** *Determination of hydrogen ion concentration (pH).*

(a) Colorimetric method

(i) Using universal pH indicator

Principle

pH indicators when mixed with water gives specific colours depending upon the pH of the sample. The colour so produced is compared with the standard colour chart.

Materials

(i) Universal pH indicator range 4.0-11.0

(ii) Test tubes

(iii) Standard colour chart

Procedure

Take 5 ml of water sample in each test tube (in replicate of two). Add 2 drops of universal indicator in each tube, shake gently. Wait for 2 minutes. Match the colour developed in the sample with the standard colour chart provided with the indicator bottle. Record the corresponding pH value. Universal indicators are commercially available.

(b) Electrometric method

Principle

Activity of hydrogen ions in a solution is measured as the difference in potentials of glass electrode over a scale calibrated directly in pH units.

Materials

(i) pH meter with combined electrode

(ii) Buffer solution of pH 4.0 and 9.2

Procedure

Keep the function switch on pH position to read 7. Wash the electrode with distilled water and dip in pH 4.0 buffer. Connect the electrode. Turn the selector switch to 0.7 pH range and adjust so that meter reads pH 4. Rinse the electrode with distilled water and blot it dry again. Repeat the calibration with a pH 9.2 buffer solution. Put the selector switch at zero, wash the electrode with distilled water and dip in the sample. Adjust temperature compensation to the temperature of the sample. Put the selector switch on 0-7 pH range. If, pH exceeds, 7, move to the other range and read it.

***Experiment 1.6** : Determination of electrical conductivity.*

The electrical conductivity of water is its capacity to conduct electric current. It is expressed as μ mhos cm^{-1}.

Materials

(i) Conductivity meter

Procedure

Take about 150 ml of water sample in a beaker and proceed according to the instructions given in the manual of conductivity meter. Express conductivity in μ mhos cm^{-1}.

***Experiment 1.7** : Determination of total dissolved solids (TDS), total suspended solids (TSS) and volatile suspended solids (VSS).*

Principle

Total dissolved solids are determined as the residue left after evaporation of the filtered samples.

Materials

(i) Evaporating dish

(ii) Hot plate/oven

(iii) Chemical balance

(iv) Desiccator

Procedure

Take a Petri dish and note its weight (A). Add to it a known volume of the filtered water sample (say 100-200 ml). Place the dish on a hot plate or in an oven (set at 105°C) for 2-3 h for complete evaporation. Remove the dish and place it in a desiccator for cooling. Note the weight again (B). Calculate the total dissolved solids (TDS) and express as mg l^{-1} as follows :

Calculations

$$\text{TDS mg } l^{-1} = \frac{\text{B-A} \times 1000 \times 1000}{V}$$

A = Initial weight of dish in grams

B = Final weight of dish in grams

V = Volume of sample taken in ml

Note : (a) For the determination of total suspended solids (TSS), use unfiltered water sample and follow the same procedure as described for TDS.

(b) For determining volatile suspended solids (VSS), ignite the residue of TSS for 1h in a muffle furnace at 550°C. Record the loss in weight.

***Experiment 1.8** : Determination of water salinity.*

(a) Argentometric method

Principle

Salinity is defined as the total weight of dissolved solids in grams contained in one litre of sea water where all organic matter is converted to oxides, all iodine and bromine is replaced by chlorine. The chlorinity is titrated with soluble silver salt in the presence of chromate, yielding relatively insoluble AgCl. An empirical relationship between salinity and chlorinity is :

Salinity (ppt) = 0.03+ 1.805 × chlorinity (ppt)

Materials

(i) Silver nitrate titrant (0.28N)

(dissolve 48.5 g $AgNO_3$ in distilled water and make the volume to 1 litre)

(ii) Potassium chromate indicator

(dissolve 63.0 g of K_2CrO_4 in distilled water and make the volume to 100 ml)

Procedure

- Bring the sample to room temperature and take 25 ml in a conical flask.
- Add to it 5 drops of potassium chromate indicator.
- Titrate it with silver nitrate titrant until yellow colour changes to brick red colour. Note the end point.

Calculations

- Calculate chlorosity (Clo)

$$\text{Clo} = \text{ml of titrant used} \times \text{Cl. Eq.} \times \frac{1000}{25}$$

Cl. Eq. = N × 0.0355

Where,

Cl. Eq. = Chlorosity equivalent of $AgNO_3$

Where,

N = normality of $AgNO_3$ titrant (0.28N)

- Convert chlorosity to chlorinity (Cl ‰) by substracting the factor given in table 210-III (See APHA 1998, pp.108).
- Substitute the value of chlorinity so obtained in the following equation :

Salinity ‰ = 0.03 + 1.805 × chlorinity ‰)

Example

Let the amount of titrant used with sample = 32.0 ml

N of $AgNO_3$ = 0.28 N

Cl Eq = 0.28 ×·0.0355

= 0.0099

$$Clo = 32.0 \times 0.0099 \times \frac{1000}{25}$$

Clo = 12.67‰

Chlorinity = 12.67 - 0.19

= 12.48‰

Salinity ‰ = 0.03 + 1.805 × 12.48 = 22.56‰

(b) Refractometer method

Now a days salinity refractometers are available which give salinity reading directly. Distilled water is used for zero adjustment. And thereafter a drop of the sample is applied for recording salinity (‰).

Experiment 1.9 : *Determination of free carbon-dioxide.*

Principle

Free CO_2 reacts with strong alkali (such as sodium hydroxide) to form bicarbonates. Completion of the reaction is indicated by the development of a pink colour, characteristic for phenolphthalein indicator.

Materials

(i) Sodium hydroxide titrant 0.02N

(0.909g NaOH in one L of CO_2 free distilled water)

(ii) Phenolphthalein indicator

(0.5g of phenolphthalein in 150 ml of ethanol (95%) and 50 ml of distilled water. Add to it 0.02N NaOH dropwise until faint pink colour appears).

Procedure

Add 2 drops of phenolphthalein indicator in a 50 ml of water sample (if slight pink colour develops then free carbon-di-oxide is absent). If the solution remains colourless, titrate using standard NaOH (0.02N) until a slight pink colour appears. Record the end point.

Calculations

$$\text{Free } CO_2 \text{ mg } l^{-1} = \frac{\text{ml of titrant used}}{\text{ml of sample taken}} \times 1000$$

Experiment 1.10 **:** *Determination of alkalinity.*

Principle

Alkalinity is estimated by titrating the sample with a standard solution of strong acid (H_2SO_4), first to pH 8.3 using phenolphthalein as an indicator (carbonate alkalinity) and then further to second end point to pH 4.5 using methyl orange as indicator (bicarbonate alkalinity).

Materials

(i) Sulphuric acid titrant 0.02N

(Dilute 2.8 ml of conc. H_2SO_4 to 1 litre-solution-A. Take 200 ml of solution A and dilute to 1 litre)

(ii) Phenolphthalein indicator

(0.5g of phenolphthalein in 50 ml of 95% ethanol and 50 ml of distilled water. Add to it 0.02N NaOH drop wise until faint pink colour appears)

(iii) Methyl orange indicator

((0.1g of Methyl orange in 200 ml of distilled water)

Procedure

- Take 50 ml of water sample in Erlenmeyer flask and add 2 drops of phenolphthalein indicator.
- If the colour changes to pink, titrate it with 0.02N H_2SO_4 until the colour disappears. Note the end point-A. This is phenolphthalein carbonate alkalinity. (If the solution remains colourless on the addition of phenolphthalein indicator, phenolphthalein alkalinity i.e. carbonates are absent).
- Now add 2-3 drops of methyl orange to the same sample and continue to titrate till the colour changes from yellow to orange. Note the amount of titrant used-'B'. This is total alkalinity.

Calculations

$$\text{Phenolphthalein alkalinity mg l}^{-1} = \frac{\text{ml of titrant 'A'}}{\text{ml of sample}} \times 1000$$

$$\text{Total alkalinity mg l}^{-1} = \frac{\text{ml of titrant 'B'}}{\text{ml of sample}} \times 1000$$

Experiment 1.11 **:** *Determination of dissolved oxygen (DO).*

Principle

Oxygen combines with divalent manganous hydroxide to form higher hydroxides, which on acidification liberate iodine equivalent to that of oxygen fixed. This iodine is titrated by standard solution of sodium thiosulphate using starch as an indicator. The presence of certain oxidizing and reducing materials interfere in the process which is removed by addition of sodium azide.

Materials

(i) Manganous sulphate solution

(Dissolve 182g of $MnSO_4$ in distilled water, filter and make the volume upto 500 ml - solution A)

(ii) Alkaline Iodide - azide solution

(a) Dissolve separately 350g KOH and 75g KI in distilled water. Mix the two solutions and make the volume upto 500 ml.

(b) Dissolve 5g sodium azide (NaN_3) in 20 ml distilled water.

Mix solution a and b - solution B

(iii) Sodium thiosulphate titrant 0.025N

(Dissolve 6.205g of $Na_2 S_2O_3$ in distilled water and make the volume to 1 litre by adding distilled water).

(iv) Starch indicator 1%

(1 g of starch in 100 ml of warm (80-90°C) distilled water.

(v) Sulphuric acid concentrated (Sp. gr. 1.84).

Procedure

Collect the water sample in 250 ml stoppered bottles, avoiding entrapping of air bubbles. Keep the bottles submerged in water. Remove the stopper and dispense 2 ml each of manganous sulphate (Solution A) and alkaline iodide-azide solutions (Solution B) one after the other, by keeping the pipettes well below the surface of water. Replace the stopper and shake the contents well by inverting the bottles. Dissolved oxygen present in the water gets precipitated in the form of yellowish brown precipitates. Allow the precipitates to settle. Dissolve the precipitates by adding 2 ml of conc. $H_2 SO_4$ and shake the stoppered bottle.

For estimation of DO, take a suitable aliquot (50 ml) in a flask and titrate against sodium thio-sulphate solution till the colour changes to pale straw. Add 2 drops of starch solution (freshly prepared) and titrate further till the blue colour disappears. Note the amount of titrant used.

Calculations

$$\text{DO in mg l}^{-1} = \frac{8 \times 1000 \times N\ (0.025) \times V'}{V}$$

Where,

V = Volume of water sample taken (ml)

V' = Volume of titrant (sodium thiosulphate) used (ml)

N = Normality of the titrant

Experiment 1.12 **:** *Determination of biochemical oxygen demand (BOD).*

Principle

The principle involves the measuring of differences in oxygen concentration in the sample before and after incubating it for 5 days (BOD_5).

Materials

(i) *Sodium thiosulphate solution (0.025N)

(ii) * Managanous sulphate solution

(iii) * Alkaline Iodide azide solution

(iv) * Starch indicator

(v) Dilution water

(Prepared by bubbling compressed air in distilled water for about 1 h. Add 1 ml each of magnesium sulphate 8.25%, anhydrous calcium chloride 2.75%, Ferric chloride 0.025% and phosphate buffer to one litre of dilution water and mix thoroughly).

(vi) Phosphate buffer (Dissolve 8.5g KH_2PO_4, 21.75g K_2HPO_4, 33.4g Na_2HPO_4 and 1.70 g NH_4Cl in distilled water. Make the volume to 1 litre by adding more distilled water. Adjust pH to 7.2)

* Prepare as described for DO determination.

Procedure

As soon as the water samples are brought to the laboratory, prepare different dilutions of the unfiltered water samples in BOD bottles (300 ml capacity) by adding dilution water according to the table 1. Prepare two sets for each dilution. Determine initial dissolved oxygen in the first set of BOD bottles and keep the second set for incubation in BOD incubator at 20°C for five days. After five days, remove the bottles from the BOD incubator and determine DO (see DO determination) from the incubated set of bottles and note the readings.

Calculations

BOD_5 in mg l^{-1} = $(D_i - D_5) \times$ dilution factor

D_i = Initial DO in the sample (mg l^{-1})

D_5 = DO after five days of incubation (mg l^{-1})

Table 1. Preparation of dilutions for various ranges of BOD in the samples

Range of BOD	Dilution (%)
0-6	No dilution
4-12	50
10-30	20
20-60	10
40-120	5
100-300	2
200-600	1
400-1200	0.5

Experiment 1.13 : Determination of chemical oxygen demand (COD).

Principle

COD is the measure of oxygen consumed during the oxidation of the oxidizable organic matter present in a water sample by a strong oxidizing agent like potassium dichromate. The sample is refluxed in a strongly acidic solution with a known amount of $K_2Cr_2O_7$. The amount of $K_2Cr_2O_7$ used is proportional to the oxidizable organic matter present in the sample.

Materials

(i) Potassium dichromate solution, 0.25N

(Dissolve 12.3g of $K_2Cr_2O_7$ AR grade in distilled water to make 1 litre of solution).

(ii) Ferrous ammonium sulphate, 0.1N

(Dissolve 39.2g of ferrous ammonium sulphate in distilled water, add 20 ml of conc. H_2SO_4. Make the volume to 1 litre.

(iii) Ferroin indicator

(It is available commercially as such, however, it can be prepared as folows : Dissolve 1.491g of 1, 10-phenanthroline and 0.695g of ferrous sulphate $FeSO_4 . 7H_2O$ in distilled water to make 100 ml of solution).

(iv) Concentrated sulphuric acid (Sp. gr. 1.84).

(v) Mercuric sulphate ($HgSO_4$ solid)

(vi) Silver sulphate (Ag_2SO_4 solid)

Procedure

Take 20ml of unfiltered water sample in COD flasks. Add 10 ml of potassium dichromate

(0.25N) solution, 30ml of sulphuric acid, and a pinch of mercuric sulphate and silver sulphate. Reflux for 2 h on a hot water bath (100°C). Cool the samples and make the volume upto 140 ml by adding distilled water. Titrate it against 0.1N ferrous ammonium sulphate solution by using 2-3 drops of ferroin indicator. Run a distilled water blank simultaneously.

Calculations

$$\text{COD mg l}^{-1} = \frac{(b-a) \times \text{N of titrant} \times 1000 \times 8}{\text{ml of sample}}$$

Where,

a = ml of titrant used with the sample

b = ml of titrant used with blank

Note : *If COD is expected below 50 mg l^{-1}, use 0.025 N of $K_2Cr_2O_7$ and 0.01 N of ferrous ammonium sulphate.*

Experiment 1.14 **:** *Determination of chlorides.*

Principle

Chloride is titrated with soluble silver nitrate in the presence of chromate, yielding precipitate of AgCl. At the end, when all the chlorides get precipitated free silver ions react with chromate to form silver chromate of reddish brown colour.

Materials

(i) Silver nitrate titrant, 0.014N

(Dissolve 2.395g of $AgNO_3$ in some distilled water and make the volume to 1 litre—Store in a dark bottle)

(ii) Potassium chromate indicator, 5%

(Dissolve 5g of K_2CrO_4 in 100 ml of distilled water)

Procedure

Add 5 drops of potassium chromate indicator to 50 ml of water sample in a conical flask. This gives yellow colour. Titrate the contents against 0.014N $AgNO_3$ until a brick red colour appears. Note the end point.

Calculations

$$\text{Chloride in mg l}^{-1} = \frac{\text{ml of titrant used} \times N \times 35.5}{\text{ml of sample (50 ml)}} \times 1000$$

N = Normality of the titrant

Experiment 1.15 : *Determination of total hardness.*

Principle

Eriochrome Black-T forms wine red complex with metal ions (Ca++ and Mg++). The disodium salt of EDTA has a stronger affinity towards Ca^{++} and Mg^{++}, therefore, by addition of EDTA, the complex is broken down and a new complex of blue colour is formed.

Materials

(i) EDTA (Ethylenediaminetetra acetic acid) titrant, 0.01N (Dissolve 3.723g of EDTA in distilled water and dilute to 1 litre. Store in plastic bottles).

(ii) Ammonia buffer solution

(Take 114 ml of conc. NH_4OH and 13.5g of NH_4Cl, make the volume upto 200 ml by adding distilled water).

(iii) Eriochrome Black-T-indicator

(0.5 g of Eriochrome Black T in 100 ml of 80% ethanol)

Procedure

Add 1 ml of ammonia buffer and 5 drops of indicator to 50 ml of water sample in a conical flask. The colour of the water sample will turn wine-red. Titrate against EDTA solution, until a blue colour appears. Note the end point.

Calculations

$$\text{Total Hardness mg l}^{-1} = \frac{\text{ml of EDTA used}}{\text{volume of sample (50 ml)}} \times 1000$$

Experiment 1.16 : *Determination of calcium.*

Calcium can be determined by titrimetric method using EDTA as titrant.

Principle

Murexide (ammonium purpurate) indicator forms pink coloured solution with Ca^{++}. When titrated with a solution of EDTA (Ethylenediaminetetra acetic acid) Ca^{++} ions forms a colourless complex with it and a purple colour solution is left.

Materials

(i) Murexide indicator.

(Mix 100mg of ammonium purpurate with 50.0g solid NaCl, grind it to a fine powder).

(ii) EDTA titrant (see as in total hardness determination).

(iii) Sodium hydroxide (8%)

(Dissolve 8.0g of NaOH pellets in distilled water and make the volume to 100 ml.)

Procedure

Take a suitable volume (say 50 ml) of the water sample in a conical flask. Add to it 2.0 ml of 8% NaOH solution and 0.2g of murexide indicator. Shake well, pink colour will appear. Titrate it against EDTA. Note the appearance of purple colour as an end point.

Calculations

$$\text{Ca mg l}^{-1} = \frac{\text{ml of titrant used} \times 400.5 \times 1.05}{\text{volume of sample taken}}$$

Experiment 1.17 : *Determination of magnesium.*

Procedure

Magnesium is determined as the differences between total hardness and calcium hardness multiplied by a factor (0.244).

Calculations

$$\text{Magnesium mg l}^{-1} = (\text{A-B}) \times 0.244$$

Where,

A = total hardness in mg l^{-1}

(as determined in section 1.15)

$$B = \frac{\text{ml of titrant used for Ca} \times 1000 \times 1.05}{\text{ml of sample taken for Ca}} = \text{Calcium hardness as } CaCO_3$$

Experiment 1.18 : *Determination of sodium and potassium.*

Sodium and potassium are the cations which naturally occur in aquatic ecosystem as well as in blood and body fluids. These can be determined accurately by flame photometry.

Experiment 1.19 : *Determination of Ammonia-nitrogen (NH_4-N).*

Principle

The ammonium ions react with alkaline solution of Nessler's reagent (Potassium mercury iodide) to form a yellow brown coloured complex of ammonium mercury iodide. The light absorption is measured at a wavelength of 425 nm.

Materials

(i) Rochelle salt solution

(Dissolve 50g of potassium sodium tartrate tetra hydrate-K $NaC_4H_4O_6.4H_2O$ in 100 ml distilled water. Remove ammonia by boiling off approximately 30 ml of the solution. After cooling, make the volume to 100 ml by adding more distilled water).

(ii) Nessler's Reagent

(Dissolve 100g HgI_2 and 70g of KI in a little distilled water-A. Dissolve 160g of NaOH in a little distilled water-B. Mix solution A and B and make the volume to 1L by adding distilled water. Store it in a rubber stoppered amber coloured bottle. Stability of this solution is 1year.

(iii) Standard stock ammonium solution

(Dissolve 0.831g anhydrous NH_4Cl (dried at 100°C) in distilled water and make the volume to 1L by adding distilled water).

(iv) Spectrophotometer

Procedure

Take 50 ml of filtered water sample in Erlenmeyer flask. Add 2 drops of Rochelle salt solution and mix well. Add 2 ml of Nessler's reagent. Wait for 10-20 minutes for colour development and take the absorbance at 425nm. Calculate the concentration of NH_4-N from the standard curve.

Note : *Use ammonia free water for preparation of all reagents.*

Standard curve

Dissolve 0.831g anhydrous NH_4 Cl (dried at 100°C) in distilled water and make the volume to 1000 ml (stock solution 100 mg l^{-1}). Take 5 ml of stock solution in a volumetric flask and make the volume 500 ml by adding distilled water (1.0 mg l^{-1}). Prepare the other standards as given below :

Standard (1 mg l^{-1}) (ml)	Distilled water (ml)	Final concentration (mg l^{-1})
0	+50	0.0
10	+40	0.2
20	+30	0.4
30	+20	0.6
40	+10	0.8

Take the absorbance at 425 nm and plot the standard curve between concentration and absorbance

Determination of ammonia by phenate method

Keeping in view the disposal problems of mercury as per the Nessler's reagent method phenate method can be employed for the estimation of ammonia.

Principle

Alkaline phenol and hypochlorite react with ammonia to form indophenol blue which is proportional to the ammonia concentration. The blue colour formed is measured at 640 nm.

Materials

(i) Phenol nitroprusside reagent :

(Dissolve 30g phenol in 1L of distilled water solution 'A'. Dissolve 1.5g of sodium nitroprusside in 100 ml distilled water -solution 'B'. Add 2 ml of B to 1L of A.)

(ii) Alkaline hypochlorite reagent

(Dissolve 10g of hypochlorite in 100 ml distilled water solution 'A'. Dissolve 20g of sodium hydroxide in 600 ml of distilled water - solution 'B'. Add 5.4 ml of A to solution B and make the volume to 1L by adding distilled water).

(iii) Standard ammonium chloride solution

(Prepare as given for the determination of NH_4-N by Nessler's reagent method)

Procedure

Take 25 ml of water sample in 50 ml erlenmeyer flask. Add, with thorough mixing, 2 ml of phenol-nitroprusside reagent, followed by 2 ml of alkaline hypochlorite reagent. Using paraffin film to cover the sample flasks. Keep the samples in dim light at temperature between 22° to 27°C. Read the absorbance at 640 nm against distilled water blank. Calculate the concentration of NH_4-N from the standard curve.

Preparation of standard curve

Same as given in Nessler's reagent method.

Experiment 1.20 **:** *Determination of nitrite-nitrogen (NO_2-N).*

Principle

In acid solution, the nitrite yields nitrous acid, which diazotises the sulphanilamide. The diazonium salt when reacts with aromatic amine, N-1, naphthyl ethylenediamine dihydrochloride forms a red azo dye, which is spectrophotometrically determined at 543 nm.

Material

(i) Sulphanilamide reagent

(Dissolve 1g sulphanilamide in 100 ml of 10% HCl)

(ii) N-1 naphthyl ethylenediamine dihydrochloride reagent

(Dissolve 0.1g in 100 ml distilled water-aromatic amine reagent)

(iii) Stock sodium nitrite solution

(Dissolve 2.46g anhydrous sodium nitrite in 1L distilled water. This is 500 mg l^{-1} standard).

Procedure

Filter the water sample through Whatman filter paper No. 1. Take 50 ml of filtered water sample and add to it 1 ml of sulphanilamide reagent. After 3 minutes, add 1 ml of aromatic amine reagent and shake thoroughly. Take the absorbance at 543 nm against a distilled water blank. Deduce the nitrite from the standard curve.

Standard curve

Dissolve 2.46g of anhydrous sodium nitrite in 1000 ml of distilled water (stock solution 500 mg l^{-1}). Take 5 ml of stock solution in a volumetric flask and make the volume 500 ml by adding distilled water (1.0 mg l^{-1}). Prepare the other standards as given below :

Standard (1.0 mg l^{-1}) (ml)	Distilled water (ml)	Final concentration (mg l^{-1})
0	+50	0.0
10	+40	0.2
20	+30	0.4
30	+20	0.6
40	+10	0.8
50	+ 0	1.0

Take the absorbance at 543 nm and plot the standard curve between concentration and absorbance.

Experiment 1.21 : *Determination of nitrate-nitrogen (NO_3-N).*

Principle

The nitrate reacts with phenol disulphonic acid to form nitro acid complex which gives yellow colour with strong alkali salt.

Materials

(i) Phenol disulphonic acid.

(ii) Potassium hydroxide 12N (Dissolve 168.2g of KOH in small quantity of distilled water and make the volume to 250 ml).

(iii) Standard potassium nitrate (stock solution)

(Dissolve 3.61g of KNO_3 in distilled water and make the volume to 500 ml).

Procedure

Evaporate 25 ml of water sample to dryness on a hot plate. Also run a blank simultaneously using distilled water. Add 0.5ml phenol disulphonic acid and dissolve the residue using a glass rod. Add to it 5 ml of distilled water, followed by 2 ml of 12N KOH. Shake and wait for 5-10 minutes. A yellow colour will develop. Take the absorbance at 410nm. Deduce the value with the help of a standard curve.

Standard curve

Dissolve 3.61g of KNO_3 in distilled water and make the volume to 500 ml-stock solution (1000 mg l^{-1}). Take 1 ml of stock solution and make the volume to 1000 ml by adding distilled water. This will give 1 mg l^{-} and prepare other dilution as follows :

Standard (1 mg l^{-1}) (ml)	Distilled water (ml)	Final concentration (mg l^{-1})
0	+50	0.0
10	+40	0.2
20	+30	0.4
30	+20	0.6
40	+10	0.8
50	+0	1.0

Take the absorbance at 410 nm and plot the standard curve between absorbance and concentration.

Experiment 1.22 : Determination of total Kjeldahl nitrogen.

Principle

Water sample is digested in strong sulphuric acid and potassium sulphate. All the amino-nitrogen and some other N-forms are converted to ammonium nitrogen and produce ammonium sulphate. The nitrogen in the form of ammonium sulphate is decomposed in alkaline medium, the resulting ammonia is distilled off, collected in a solution of boric acid and determined by acid titration.

Materials

(i) Sulphuric acid conc. (Sp. gr. 1.84)

(ii) Copper sulphate solution, 10%
(10g $CuSO_4$ in 100 ml of distilled water)

(iii) NaCl solution, 10%
(10g of NaCl in 100 ml of distilled water)

(iv) Potassium sulphate AR grade
(K_2SO_4 solid)

(v) Sodium hydroxide, 10N

(40g of NaOH in distilled water and make the volume to 100 ml)

(vi) Hydrochloric acid titrant, 0.01N

(Add 0.5 ml conc. HCl to 600 ml of distilled water)

(vii) Boric acid + mixed indicator

(Dissolve 20g Boric acid in 900 ml distilled water + 100 ml ethanol (95%) - I.

Dissolve 0.5 gm of Bromocresol green and 0.1g methyl red in 100 ml of 95% ethanol and neutralize to mid colour (Bluish purple) with a few drops of 10N NaOH-II).

(Add 10 ml of solution II to solution I).

(viii) Micro kjeldahl assembly

Procedure

Take 40 ml of water sample in a 100 ml flask. Add to it 4 ml conc. H_2SO_4, 0.3 ml of $CuSO_4$, 6.0 g of solid K_2SO_4 and 1 ml of 10% NaCl. Heat the flask on a hot plate for digesting the samples till the colour of the sample turns pale green, continue heating for another 30 minutes. Cool the flask and make up the volume to 100 ml by adding distilled water.

Take 25 ml of the digest, add 10 ml of 10N NaOH and distill the sample using micro kjeldahl's apparatus. Collect the gas in a conical flask containing 5 ml of boric acid + mixed indicator, continue the distillation till about 40 ml of distillate is collected. Titrate the distillate with 0.01 N HCl till the colour changes from blue to brcwn or faint pink.

Run a distilled water blank simultaneously.

Calculations

$$\text{Kjeldahl N- mg l}^{-1} = \frac{\text{a-b} \times 1000 \times 0.14 \times D}{\text{ml of sample distilled}}$$

Where,

a = ml of HCl used with sample

b = ml of HCl used with blank

D = dilution factor (Since the original volume of 40 ml of the sample has been made to 100 ml after digestion hence dilution factor is 2.5).

***Experiment 1.23** : Determination of Orthophosphate (Soluble reactive phosphorous).*

Principle

The Orthophosphate ($O\text{-}PO_4$) reacts with acidified ammonium molybdate solution and form molybdophosphoric acid, which is then reduced to a blue complex in the presence of stannous chloride. This is measured spectrophotometrically at 690 nm.

Materials

(i) Ammonium molybdate strong acid solution

(Dissolve 5g of Ammonium Molybdate $(NH_4)_6\ Mo_7O_{24}.\ 4H_2O$) in 35 ml of distilled water. Add 62 ml of conc. H_2SO_4 to 80 ml of distilled water, cool and add the molybdate solution and make the volume to 200 ml by adding more distilled water).

(ii) Stannous chloride solution

(Dissolve 0.5g $SnCl_2.\ 2H_2O$ in 2 ml conc. HCl. Make the volume to 20 ml with distilled water).

(iii) Stock phosphate solution for standard curve

(Dissolve 219.5 mg anhydrous KH_2PO_4 in 1000 ml distilled water-stock solution).

(iv) Spectrophotometer

Procedure

Take 25 ml of the water sample in a conical flask (100 ml). Also run a distilled water blank simultaneously. Add 1 ml ammonium molybdate solution, 3 drops stannous chloride solution and shake the contents. Blue colour will appear, wait for 10 minutes and take the reading on spectrophotometer at 690 nm. Deduce the value of O-PO_4 mg l^{-1} with the help of a standard curve.

Standard curve

Dissolve 219.5 mg of KH_2PO_4 in distilled water and make the volume upto 1000 ml (stock solution-50 mg/litre). Take 10 ml of stock phosphate solution in a volumetric flask and make the volume to 500 ml by adding distilled water (1.0 mg l^{-1}). Prepare the other standards as given below :

Standard solution 1.0 mg l^{-1} (ml)	Distilled water (ml)	Final concentration (mg l^{-1})
0	+50	0.0
10	+40	0.2
20	+30	0.4
30	+20	0.6
40	+10	0.8
50	+0	1.0

Take the absorbance at 690 nm and plot the standard curve between concentration and absorbance.

***Experiment 1.24** : Determination of total phosphate.*

Principle

All forms of phosphorus viz. soluble reactive phosphate, polyphosphate, organic phosphate are converted to soluble inorganic orthophosphate by digestion with perchloric acid and oxidation with sodium hydroxide.

Materials

(i) Perchloric acid AR grade 60% or 70%

(ii) Phenolphthalein indicator
(see free CO_2 determination)

(iii) Sodium hydroxide 8%
(Dissolve 8 g of NaOH in 100 ml of distilled water).

(iv) Other reagents as for Orthophosphate determination.

Procedure

Evaporate a known volume (say 25 ml) of water sample to dryness in a 100 ml conical flask. Cool and add 1 ml of perchloric acid, shake the flask gradually so that the residue gets completely covered with the acid. Gently heat the flask on a hot plate till the residue is colourless. Increase the temperature to evaporate the perchloric acid. Do not allow to dry. Allow the residue to cool and add 100 ml of distilled water and then add one drop of phenolphthalein indicator. Titrate against 8% NaOH solution until slight pink colour is just restored. With these treatments all forms of phosphate are converted into orthophosphate. Now make the volume to 25 ml by adding distilled water and proceed to determine orthophosphate spectrophotometrically as described earlier (experiment No. 1.23). Deduce the value from a standard curve. This willl give total phosphate mg l^{-1}.

***Experiment 1.25** : Determination of sulphate.*

Principle

Sulphate ions are precipitated in a hydrochloric acid (HCl) medium with barium chloride ($BaCl_2$) so as to form barium sulphate ($BaSO_4$) crystals of uniform size. Light absorbance of $BaSO_4$ is measured spectrophotometrically at 420 nm against a standard curve.

Materials

(i) Spectrophotometer

(ii) Barium chloride

(iii) NaCl-HCl solution
(Dissolve 120g of NaCl in 450 ml of distilled water, add 10 ml of HCl and make the volume to 500 ml by adding more distilled water)

(iv) Glycerol-ethanol solution

(Add 100 ml of glycerol to 200 ml of ethyl alcohol)

Procedure

- Filter the water sample through Whatman filter paper No. 1.
- Take 50 ml of the filtered sample.
- Add to it 10 ml each of NaCl-HCl solution and glycerol-ethanol solution one after the other.
- Add 0.15g of barium chloride and mix for 30 minutes on magnetic stirrer.
- Note the absorbance at 420 nm against a distilled water blank.

Standard curve

Standard sulphate solution

Dissolve 0.1479g of anhydrous sodium sulphate in distilled water and make the volume to 1L. This solution contains 100 mg l^{-1} of sulphate. Prepare the other concentrations as follows:

Standard solution 100.0 mg l^{-1} (ml)	Distilled water (ml)	Final concentration (mg l^{-1})
0.0	+50.0	0.0
10.0	+40.0	20.0
20.0	+30.0	40.0
30.0	+20.0	60.0
40.0	+10.0	80.0
50.0	+00.0	100.0

Take the absorbance at 420 nm and plot the standard curve between concentration and absorbance.

SEDIMENT ANALYSIS

Collection and preservation of sediment samples

Sediment samples are collected in polythene bags. Percentage moisture, electrical conductivity and pH is determined immediately, whereas, for other physico-chemical parameters sediment is left to dry at air temperature.

Experiment 1.26 : *Write notes on (a) cone sampler (b) Ekman's dredge.*

(a) Cone Sampler

This sampler has a cone shaped metallic cup with sharp cutting edge. The cone is attached to a light weight iron rod having a handle at one end (Fig. 1.4). For the collection of sediment sample, the cone is dragged over the bottom sediment with the help of a string or rope. After covering a suitable distance the sampler is lifted. In order to know the volume of the sediment collected, calculate the volume of the cone by geometrical formula $(\pi r^2 h)/3$, where r is the radius and h is height. This sampler is useful for collecting sediment samples from shallow water bodies.

(b) Ekman's Dredge

This is widely used for the collection of sediment samples from deep waters. It consists of a metallic box with two jaws at the bottom. The jaws remain closed under the tension of a spring (Fig. 1.5). The box is lowered in the water body with jaws in open position. When open jaws touches the bottom of the water body, sediment is grabbed. At the same time weight is dropped along the rope which results in the closure of jaws and the bottom sediment gets enclosed in the box. The Ekman's dredge is then lifted along the sample. For calculating the volume of the sediment collected, determine the volume of the box of the dredge.

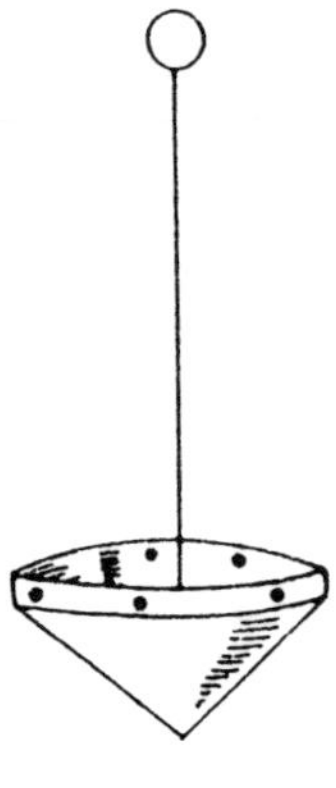

Fig. 1.4. Cone sampler.

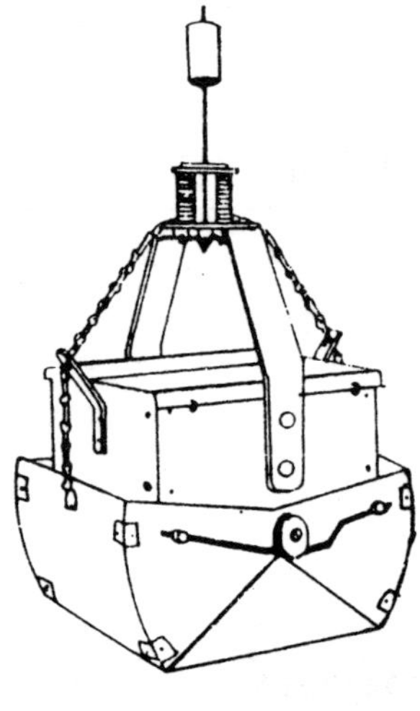

Fig. 1.5. Ekman's dredge.

Physico-chemical characteristics of sediment/soil

Soil is an important component of a pond bottom for conservation and release of nutrients.

Experiment 1.27 : *Determination of soil texture by gravimetric method.*

Materials

(i) Hydrogen peroxide

(ii) 1N Hydrochloric acid

(iii) 1N sodium hydroxide

cedure

- Collect the soil sample using Ekman's dredge/cone sampler from different areas of the bottom of the pond or lake etc.
- Dry the soil sample in shade, when dry grind the soil and determine soil texture as follows :

Take 20 g of soil sample in 400 ml beaker + 35 ml H_2O_2 → Heat on a water bath (100°C) till frothing stops → Cool and add 50 ml of 1 N HCl + 200 ml distilled water

↓ Allow to stand for 1 h with occassional stirring

Filter using a filter paper → Wash with hot water → Transfer the residue to 1 L beaker → Add 8.0 ml of 1 N NaOH

↓ ke for 20 utes on a hanical ær

Transfer the contents to a 1 L measuring cylinder → Shake vigrously for one minute → Allow to stand for 4 minutes → Dip a 20 ml pipette with tip 10 cm deep → Suck 20 ml contents

↓

Dry in 50 ml beaker → Note the weight of clay+silt (a) → Wait for 2 h → Again dip the Pipette with tip 10 cm deep and suck 20 ml content → the contents in nl beaker and note weight of clay (b)

|

:ulate the % of sand, and clay separately

:ulations

% of sand = 100 - (% of clay + silt)

% of silt = a-b

e : *A special type of hydrometer graduated in g l^{-1} can also be used for determining the percentage of suspended matter when 100 g of soil is taken*

Experiment 1.28 **:** *Determination of moisture contents of soil sample.*

Materials

(i) Balance

(ii) Oven

(iii) Grinder/homogenizer

(iv) Petridishes

Procedure

- Take a petridish, record its weight (A)
- Take a weighed amount of freshly collected sediment sample in the petridish (B).
- Place the petridish for 24h in an oven maintained at 105°C for drying the sample.
- Remove the petridish from the oven, allow it to cool then again record the weight (C). Calculate the loss in weight. This will give the per cent moisture contents.

Calculations

$$\text{Moisture contents \%} = \frac{A+B-C}{A+B} \times 100$$

Experiment 1.29 **:** *Determination of soil pH.*

Materials

Freshly collected sediment sample. Distilled water and all other materials as required for the determination of water pH.

Procedure

Prepare 1:5 or 1:10 suspension of sediment w/v in distilled water. Determine pH by using pH meter or pH indicator paper or pH indicator solution.

Experiment 1.30 **:** *Determination of electrical conductivity (EC)*

Materials

(i) Conductivity meter

Procedure

Prepare a fresh suspension of mud (1:10) and determine conductivity immediately using conductivity meter.

Experiment 1.31 **:** *Determination of soil alkalinity and chlorides.*

Materials

(i) Freshly collected sediment sample

(ii) Whatman filter paper No. 40

Procedure

- Prepare 1:10 suspension of soil by taking 10 g of sediment in 100 ml of distilled water. Filter the suspension using Whatman filter paper No. 40.
- Determine total alkalinity and chlorides from the suspension following the procedure as described for water analysis. Calculate as follows :

$$\text{Alkalinity/chlorides mg g}^{-1} = \frac{A}{10} \times \frac{V}{W(100\text{-}M)}$$

Where,

A = Value of alkalinity/chlorides in the filtrate (mg l^{-1})

V = Total volume of mud suspension (ml)

W = Weight of fresh mud taken (g)

M = Moisture contents of fresh sediment (%)

Experiment 1.32 : *Determination of soluble phosphate (Orthophosphate) in sediment.*

Principle

The soluble orthophosphate in soil can be determined in the acidic extract following the method as described for water analysis.

Materials

(i) Whatman filter paper No. 40

(ii) Sulphuric acid, 0.002 N

(Take 1.4 ml of conc. H_2SO_4 and make the volume to 500 ml using distilled water -A. Take 10 ml of 'A' and make the volume to 500 ml. Add 3.0g of potassium sulphate to it).

(iii) For all other reagents see determination of orthophosphate in water samples.

Procedure

Take 1g of air dried and powdered soil in 500 ml conical flask and add 200 ml of 0.002N H_2SO_4. Shake the suspension on magnetic shaker for about 30 minutes. Filter through Whatman filter paper No. 40. Use the filtrate for O-PO_4 determination following the procedure as described for water analysis.

Calculations

$$\text{O-PO}_4\text{mg g}^{-1} = \frac{\text{Value of orthophosphate in filtrate}}{10000} \times \frac{\text{Volume of suspension}}{\text{Wt. of dried mud sample taken}}$$

***Experiment 1.33** : Determination of nitrate in sediment*

Principle

Copper sulphate extracts the nitrate from soil in suspension. With phenoldisulphonic acid and strong alkali, yields yellow colour which is colorometrically measured at 410 nm.

Materials

(i) Nitrate extraction solution (NES)

(Dissolve 2.5g of $CuSO_4 . H_2O$ in distilled water and make the volume upto 20 ml (1 N $CuSO_4$ solution) -'A'. Dissolve 0.6g of $Ag_2 SO_4$ in 100 ml of distilled water (0.6% silver sulphate solution) -'B'.

Mix A and B and dilute to 1000 ml.

(ii) Calcium hydroxide-solid.

(iii) Magnesium carbonate-solid.

(iv) For other reagents see determination of NO_3 in water.

Procedure

Take 25g of air dried sediment in a flask. Add to it 125ml of NES. Shake well for about 15 minutes. Add 0.2g of Ca $(OH)_2$ and shake further for about 5 minutes and then add a pinch of Mg CO_3 (about 0.5g). Filter the solution. Discard first 20ml of filtrate. Evaporate 25-50 ml of the remaining filtrate to dryness and proceed for nitrate determination, employing the same procedure as already described for water. Run a distilled water blank simultaneously.

Calculations

$$NO_3\text{-N mg g}^{-1} = \frac{a \times V}{1000 \times W}$$

Where,

a = NO_3-N in the filtrate (mg l^{-1})

V = Volume of total soil extract

W = Weight of dried mud sample (g)

***Experiment 1.34** : Determination of organic matter.*

Materials

(i) Potassium dichromate solution, 1 N

(Take 24.5 g of $K_2 Cr_2O_7$, dissolve in distilled water and make the volume to 500 ml)

(ii) Sulphuric acid concentrated

(iii) Phosphoric acid

(iv) Diphenylamine indicator

(Dissolve 0.5g diphenylamine in 20 ml of distilled water.Add 100ml of H_2SO_4.)

(v) Ferrous ammonium sulphate, 0.5N

(Dissolve 196.1g Fe $(NH_4)_2$ $(SO_4)_2$ in distilled water containing 20 ml conc. H_2SO_4. Make the volume to 1000 ml).

Procedure

Take a known quantity (approx. 2g) of oven dried, finely powdered soil in a flask. Add to it 10 ml of $K_2Cr_2O_7$ solution (1N), and 15ml of conc. H_2SO_4 with continuous shaking. Keep the solution for about 20 minutes and thereafter make the volume upto 200 ml by adding more distilled water. Add 10 ml of phosphoric acid and 1 ml of diphenylamine indicator and a pinch of sodium flouride. Shake and titrate with 0.5N ferrous ammonium sulphate solution till bright green colour appears. Run a distilled water blank simultaneously.

Calculations

$$\frac{6.7}{\text{Wt. of soil sample taken}} \times \frac{(1\text{-A})}{\text{B}} = \%\ \text{organic matter}$$

A = Volume of titrant used for sample
B = Volume of titrant used for blank

Note : *For detecting heavy metals from water/sediment samples use of atomic absorption spectrophotometer (AAS) is recommended.*

Biological characteristics of water

Collection and preservation of water sample for qualitative and quantitative analysis of planktons

(a) Using plankton net

The most common method for the collection of plankton is the filtration of known amount of water sample (taken from different locations of water body) through a plankton net (Fig. 1.6) of known mesh (50-125 μm mesh size). The concentrated samples are then carefully transferred to a measuring cylinder and made upto a standard vaolume (50-100 ml) with distilled water. Samples are preserved in small plastic bottles with 5% buffered formalin. Many minute algae (e.g. nanoplankton) sometimes pass through the pores of the net resulting in under estimations of population density. Therefore, concentration of the phytoplanktons in a water sample by sedimentation is a better method for the accurate qualitative and quantitative analysis.

(b) By sedimentation method (for phytoplankton only)

Take one litre of water sample in a glass beaker.

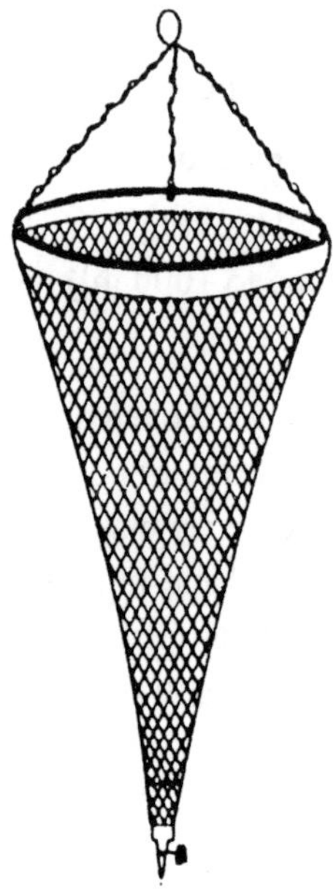

Fig. 1.6. Plankton net.

- Add 10 ml of Lugol's iodine (for preparing Lugol's Iodine solution, dissolve 10g of neutral potassium iodide in 20ml of distilled water - solution 'A'. Add 5g of iodine crystals and 5g of sodium acetate to 50 ml of distilled water-solution 'B'. Mix solution A and B) and allow it to stand for at least 24 hours to ensure complete sedimentation.
- Remove the supernatent with the help of a pipette and further concentrate the remaining sample to 20 to 100 ml (depending upon the number of plankton) by centrifugation.

***Experiment 1.35 :** Identify and count the number of planktons (species wise) in the given water sample by (a) drop count method and also by using (b) Sedgwick Rafter cell.*

(a) Drop count method

This is the simplest method for counting planktons and is reliable especially when plankton density is high.

Materials

(i) Compound microscope

(ii) Microslides (glass slides), cover slips, standard dropper

Procedure

Shake the concentrated sample and put exactly one drop onto a glass slide. Place a cover slip carefully and observe it under the microscope. Count phytoplankton species wise and make record (Table 2). Move the slide from one corner to another, counting the phytoplankton in each visible field. In this way observe the whole slide. Observe 3-6 drops to avoid error.

Observation

Date of collection :

Original volume of sample :

Volume of concentrated sample :

No. of drops in 1 ml :

Volume of one drop :

Table 2. Observation table

S.No.	Name of the plankton species	No. of plankton/drop			Average No. of plankton per drop
		1	2	3	
1.					
2.					
3.					
4.					

Calculations

$$\text{Plankton } l^{-1} = \frac{\text{Number of organisms per drop} \times \text{Volume of concentrated sample in ml}}{\text{Volume of original sample in litres} \times \text{Volume of one drop (ml)}}$$

(b) Sedgwick-Rafter cell (Fig. 1.7)

Sedgwick-Rafter cell is a rectangular cavity in the glass slide (50×20×1 mm) having 1 ml (1000 mm^3) capacity. The floor of the cavity is divided into areas of 1 cubic mm squares.

Materials

Compound microscope, Sedgwick Rafter cell, cover glass, pipettes.

Procedure

- Shake the concentrated sample and transfer one ml into the cell cavity.
- Place the cover slip on the cell carefully, avoiding bubbles and allow a time of 15 minutes for planktons to settle.
- Count plankton on 10 randomly selected fields of chamber under microscope.
- Repeat the experiment for a minimum of five samples.

No. of planktons l^{-1} = (P×C×100)/L

Where, P = the number of plankton counted in ten fields; C= volume of final concentrate of sample (ml) and L = the volume of water sample (L)

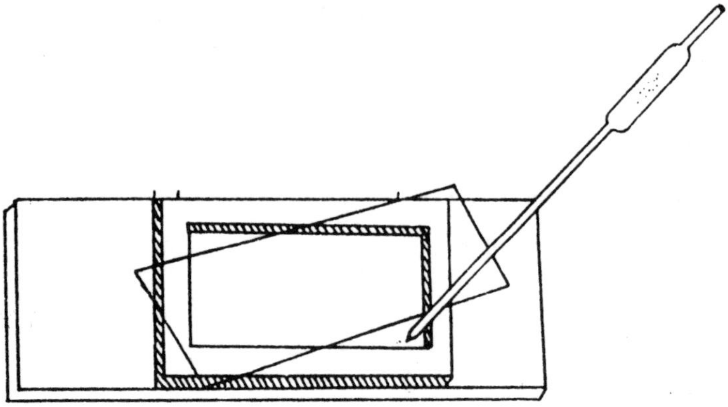

Fig. 1.7. Sedgwick Rafter cell.

Experiment 1.36 **:** *Collect a periphyton sample from the fish pond, identify and count*:

Periphyton are small sessile biota which grow on submerged objects such as rocks, stones, on sand, sediment, plants or on animal surfaces etc. Along with phytoplankton, they act as an additional food source for many of the aquaculturally important fish species.

Materials

Microscope slides, scalpel, plankton bottles, formaline/Lugol's iodine solution.

Procedure

Students can remove the submerged stones, wooden pieces, submerged plants or scrap the sides of the ponds. Scrap, collect and preserve the periphyton samples in 5% formaline or in 2-3 drops of Lugol's Iodine solution and observe the various groups of periphyton. Shake well the preserved sample. Use drop count method (as described for phytoplankton) for counting periphyton populations.

Experiment 1.37 **:** *Determination of species diversity index of biotic populations.*

Several indices are used to calculate species diversity of phytoplankton, zooplankton and benthic fauna :

(a) **Marglef's species diversity index** (Marglef, 1958)

$$\bar{d} = \frac{S-1}{\log N}$$

Where,

$\bar{d}$ = Species diversity

S = Total number of species

N = Total number of individuals present in a sample (population)

(b) Shannon and Weaver's Diversity Index (Shannon & Weaver, 1963; Washington,1984)

This gives a better understanding of biotic diversity since every species is taken into consideration.

$$\bar{d} = -\Sigma\,(ni/N)\,\log_2 ni/N$$

Where,

$\bar{d}$ = Species diversity

ni = Number of individuals of ith species

N = Total number of individuals in the sample

Experiment 1.38 **:** *Determination of primary productivity of pond water.*

The total assimilation rate of producers in an ecosystem is designated as primary productivity. It is the total amount of organic matter fixed including that used in respiration during the measurement period (Net Primary Productivity (NPP) is the rate of accumulation of new organic matter per unit time).

There are several methods for the determination of primary productivity :

(a) Light and dark bottle method

Principle

The amount of CO_2 consumed during photosynthetic activity is directly proportional to the amount of oxygen liberated which is determined by modified Winkler's method for DO determination.

Materials

(i) Glass stoppered transparent BOD Bottles-300 ml capacity-light bottles -LB

(ii) Amber coloured/blackened BOD bottles-300 ml capacity-Dark bottles-DB

(iii) Rope/thread

(iv) All other materials/chemicals as required for DO determinations

Procedure

- Before proceeding for the determination of primary productivity of a water body, collect and fix samples for DO determinations as described earlier.
- Take a set of light bottles (LB) and a set of Dark bottles (DB) for replicate sampling.
- Fill both the sets of bottles with water sample for DO determination, stopper them tightly and hang them at a desired depth for a period of 24 h in the same water body at a fixed depth.
- Remove the bottles, fix and analyse DO as described earlier.
- Calculate as follows.

Calculation

Net oxygen productivity (NOP) (mg l^{-1}) = LB-LIB

Gross oxygen productivity (GOP) (mg l^{-1}) = LB-DB

Oxygen consumed in community respiration (OCR) (mg l^{-1}) = LIB-DB

Where,

LB = DO concentration of the sample in light bottle after 24h of incubation in mg l^{-1}.

DB = DO concentration of the sample in dark bottle after 24 h of incubation mg l^{-1}.

LIB = DO concentration of the sample in the beginning of the experiment mg l^{-1}.

Net primary productivity(NPP), Gross primary productivity and community respiration (CR) can be converted and expressed in g C m^{-3} d^{-1} by multiplying GOP, NOP and OCR respectively with a factor 0.375 and dividing the products by the period of incubation in days.

$$\text{NPP g C m}^{-3}\ \text{d}^{-1} = \frac{\text{NOP} \times 0.375}{t}$$

$$\text{GPP g C m}^{-3}\ \text{d}^{-1} = \frac{\text{GOP} \times 0.375}{t}$$

$$\text{CR g C m}^{-3}\ \text{d}^{-1} = \frac{\text{OCR} \times 0.375}{t}$$

Where,

t = Period of incubation in days

Note : g Cm^{-3} d^{-1} = mg C $l^{-1}d^{-1}$

1 mole of O_2 (32g) is released for each mole of carbon (12g) fixed, therefore factor, is 12/32 = 0.375.

(b) By studying diurnal changes in DO concentrations

Dissolved oxygen (DO) contents in a water body keep on changing over a 24 hour period, therefore, determination of DO concentrations at short and regular intervals (say every 3 h) could provide an insight into the productivity of the aquatic ecosystem. DO concentration is minimum during early morning-increasing during the day time, reaching its peak during the afternoon, declining again during the night time.

Materials

(i) DO bottles and all chemicals as required for DO determination

Procedure

Collect and fix DO samples at regular intervals (say every 3-4 h) during the day and analyse as described earlier.

Calculation

Net oxygen productivity = $DO_{t_2} - DO_{t_1} / \Delta t$

Rate of respiration = $(DO_{t_1} - DO_{r_2}) / \Delta t$

Where,

DO_{t_1} = Oxygen concentration (mg l^{-1}) at time t_1

DO_{t_2} = Oxygen concentration at time t_2

Δt = Time interval in hours between two samplings viz. DO_{t_1} and DO_{t_2}.

Presume that the rate of the respiration during day hours is approximately the same as during the night hours, then the gross oxygen productivity (GOP) will be :

GOP (mg $O_2 l^{-1} h^{-1}$) = Net oxygen productivity + rate of respiration

(c) By ^{14}C technique

In this method primary productivity is determined by using the radioactive isotope ^{14}C as a tracer.

Materials

(i) Borosilicate glass bottles for collecting water sample.

(ii) pH indicator

(iii) Phenolphthalein indicator

(iv) Methyl orange indicator

(v) N/50 H_2SO_4 titrant

(vi) NaOH titrant

(vii) Borosilicate light and dark bottles (300 ml capacity)

(viii) Sodium bicarbonate containing ^{14}C

(ix) Millipore filtration assembly

(x) Hydrochloric acid

(xi) Scintillation liquid/fluid

(Take 400 ml xylene, 400 ml dioxane, 200 ml ethyl alcohol, PPO 2.5g and POPOP 0.5g and mix)

Procedure

- Collect the water samples from different depths and determine pH, total alkalinity and free CO_2 according to the methods already described.
- Fill 3 borosilicate glass bottles (2 light and 1 dark) with the water sample and add a measured quantity (say 5 μci ^{14}C/ml) of sodium bicarbonate containing ^{14}C.

- Seal the bottles and suspend in water (pond etc.) for a fixed duration of 3-4 hours.
- Remove the bottles at the end of incubation period and take these to the laboratory.
- Filter the water sample and collect the phytoplankton on a membrane filter paper using millipore filtration unit by applying pressure of about 0.5 atmosphere.
- Treat the filter paper in HCl fumes for 20 minutes to remove excess of ^{14}C and then place the filter paper in a vial containing 5 ml of Scintillation fluid.
- Take the counts using a liquid scintillation counter (β radiation).

Calculations

Total alkalinity = T

Free CO_2 = A

Bicarbonate alkalinity = $\frac{T-5 \times 10^{pH-10}}{1+0.94 \times 10^{pH-10}} = B$

Carbonate alkalinity = $0.9 \times B \times 10^{pH-10} = C$

Then total CO_2 = A + 0.44 (2B+C) in water

Sodium bicarbonate content in the radioactive ampoule = D

Then total CO_2 = A + 0.44 (2B+C) + D = E

Total inorganic carbon = $\frac{12}{44} \times E = F$

Now if the light bottle counts = X_1

Dark bottle counts = X_2

Total volume of bottle = X_3

Volume filtered = X_4

Time of incubation = X_5

Total radio-activity added to each bottle = X_6

Efficiency of the counter X_7 = appx. 40%

Then net primary production mg C/m³ h = $$\frac{(X_1-X_2) \times \frac{X_3}{X_4} \times 1.064 \times 100 \times F}{X_5 \times X_6 \times X_7}$$

Where,

1.064 is a correction factor for isotope effect

(d) Through estimation of bacterial populations

Bacteria play an important role in the degradation/ mineralization of organic and inorganic wastes in the water body. Bacterial load, therefore, is directly proportional to nutrient availability and consequently to the availability of fish food organisms. Productive water possess a bacterial load of about 10^2 - 10^3 ml^{-1}, while polluted waters have a bacterial load of about 10^4 ml^{-1} or above. Bacterial load below 10 ml^{-1} is an indicator of low productivity (Das, 1997).

Materials

(i) Nutrient Agar medium

(Composition : Tryptone - 5.0g; Yeast extract : 2.0g; Glucose 2.0g; Agar 15.0g; Distilled water - 1000ml and pH 7.0±0.1).

(ii) Autoclave for sterilization

(iii) Laminar flow

(iv) Sterilized petriplates, pipettes (1 ml and 0.1 ml), Bunsen burner/spirit lamp, Spreader

Methodology

It can be measured by standard plate count technique-SPC (APHA, 1998) as follows :

Procedure

- Collect the water samples in pre-sterilized bottles from a known depth.
- Select dilutions according to the expected SPC. Generally-undiluted sample (1:0), diluted to 10 times (1:10), 100 times (1:100), 1000 times (1:1000) are prepared by the serial dilution technique.
- Label the bottom of autoclaved petriplates.
- Pour 15-20 ml of lukewarm nutrient agar medium in each petridish.
- Gently rotate the plate to distribute the medium evenly and allow the medium to solidify.
- Thereafter, transfer 0.1 ml of the serially diluted samples to the plates with the help of a micropipette.
- Take the glass spreader, dip it in alcohol and then heat it in the flame and use it for spreading the sample on the plate.
- Incubate the plate at 28.0°C±2.0°C for 36-48 hours and keep them inverted.
- After incubation (for 36-48 h), count the colonies in each plate and calculate SPC ml^{-1} as follows :

Table 3. Observation table to record standard plate count

S.No.	Dilution	Dilution factor	SPC ml^{-1} I	SPC ml^{-1} II	SPC ml^{-1} III	Mean SPC
1.	1:0	1.0				
2.	1:10	0.1				
3.	1:100	0.01				
4.	1:1000	0.001				

Calculations

$$\text{SPC ml}^{-1} = \frac{\text{Colonies counted}}{\text{Dilution factor}}$$

Range of productivity of water

10^2 - 10^3 ml^{-1} - Productive

> 10^4 ml^{-1} - Polluted

< 10 ml^{-1} - Low productive

Serial Dilution Technique

- Prepare dilution blanks by taking 9 ml distilled water in each test tube.
- Transfer 1 ml of the sample to a 9 ml dilution blank aseptically. Mix the contents. This is 1:10 or 10^{-1} dilution.
- Using a fresh pipette, transfer 1 ml of 1:10 dilution to another 9 ml dilution blank' this is 1:100 or 10^{-2} dilution.
- Repeat the process still a desired dilution is obtained as follows :

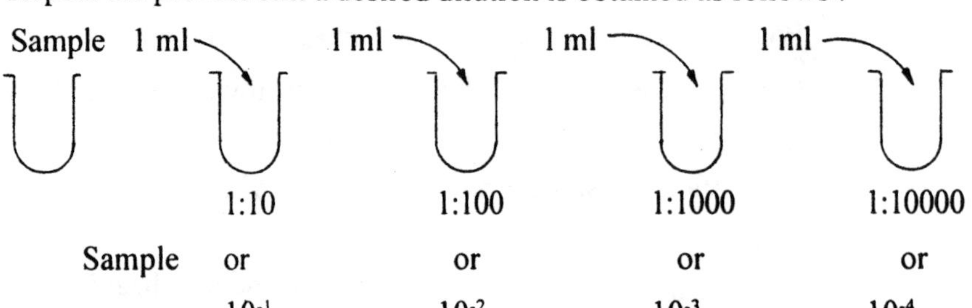

(e) **By phosphate estimation method**

- Estimate the initial available phosphate concentration from the water sample (as described earlier).

- Take 250 or 500 ml bottle, fill it with water sample and incubate the same for a period of 4h (normally between 10:00 to 14 : 00h). At the end of incubation, remove the bottles and estimate orthophosphate.
- Calculate the carbon fixation rate and consequently the primary productivity as follows :
  - Initial phosphate reading
  - Final phosphate reading
  - Difference

For each mg consumption of phosphorus 50 mg of carbon is fixed.

Experiment 1.39 : *Determination of chlorophyll a, b and c from the given water sample.*

Principle

The pigments are extracted using aqueous acetone from the concentrated plankton sample. The amount of chlorophyll pigments dissolved are proportional to the absorbance in the spectrophotometer at a wave length ranging from 630 to 750 nm.

Materials

(i) Aqueous Acetone solution (90%)

(ii) 1% $MgCO_3$ (Dissolve 1.0g finely powdered $MgCO_3$ in 100ml of distilled water).

(iii) Tissue grinder/pestle mortar/homogenizer

(iv) Centrifuge

(v) Spectrophotometer

Procedure

- Filter a known volume (say about 500 ml-1000 ml) of water sample using Whatman filter paper No. 40 under suction pressure.
- Roll the filter paper and put it in plastic tubes.
- Add sufficient measured volume (say 5-10ml) of 90% acetone (ice-cold)/ methanol/ethanol so as to cover the filter paper.
- Add 0.2 ml Mg CO_3 to prevent degradation of pigments.
- Ground the filter paper using tissue grinder.
- Add again 5 ml of 90% acetone and stir.
- Cover the tubes and keep them in a refrigerator for 24h (if acetone is used).
- If the solvent is ethanol or methanol, heat the tubes (under dim light) to near boiling.
- Centrifuge the tubes at 3000 rpm for 10 minutes.
- Decant the supernatant into glass cuvettes.

- Note the absorbance at 630 nm, 647 nm, 664 nm and 750 nm wave lengths Adjust zero with distilled water.

Note 1. *Filter only 100 ml of water, if highly green algal rich.*
2. *Time for extraction be kept constant for all the samples from one area.*

Calculations

Chlorophyll a, b and c can be calculated by inserting the absorbance values obtained at wave lengths 630, 647 and 664 nm in the following equations (APHA, 1998).

$$\text{Chlorophyll a mg l}^{-1} = 11.85\,(664) - 1.54\,(647) - 0.08\,(630)$$

$$\text{Chlorophyll b mg l}^{-1} = 21.03\,(647) - 5.43\,(664) - 2.66\,(630)$$

$$\text{Chlorophyll c mg l}^{-1} = 24.52\,(630) - 7.60\,(647) - 1.67\,(664)$$

Where,

664, 647 and 630 are absorbances (optimal densities with a 1 cm light path at the respective wave lengths).

Amount of pigment per unit volume is calculated as :

$$\text{Chlorophyll a/b/c mg/m}^3 = \frac{\text{Chl. a/b/c} \times \text{Volume of acetone extract}}{\text{Volume of the sample (L)}}$$

If pheophytin 'a' is to be determined :

- After recording the concentration of chlorophyll a, b & C acidify the samples by adding 0.1 ml of 0.1 N HCl.
- Record the absorbance at 750 and 665 nm after 90 seconds of acidification and calculate as follows :

$$\text{Pheophytin a (mg/m}^3) = \frac{[26.7 \times \{1.7(665a) - 664b\} \times \text{Volume of extract}]}{\text{Volume of sample, m}^3}$$

Note : Substract the absorbance values recorded at 750 nm (correction factor for turbidity) from all other absorbance values recorded at 630, 647, 664 and 665 nm before calculations.

IDENTIFICATION OF COMMON PLANKTONS (see plates 1 to 4)

Phytoplanktons

These are Chlorophyll bearing suspended particles consisting of members of Chlorophyceae, Euglenophyceae, Bacillariophyceae, Cyanophyceae and Dinophyceae. Identifying characters of common species are given below :

1. *Chlorophyceae*

This includes green algae and generally occur in fresh waters. They may be unicellular filamentous, colonial or coenobial. Cell-wall is made of cellulose.

Chlamydomonas

Unicellular, spherical/oval shaped motile cell.

- Two flagellae are visible at the anterior end.
- A blepharoplast or basal granule is present at the base of each flagellum.
- Chloroplast cup shaped.
- Eye spot known as stigma is present.

Volvox

- Thallus is multicellular, motile and coenobial.
- Colony pin head shaped, green in colour, containing about 400 cells and appear like a hollow sphere.
- Cells biflagellate may be globose or pyriform and are seen arranged at the periphery.
- Each cell possess a distinct gelatinous envelope.
- Flagellae are visible at the periphery of the colony.

Sphaerocystis

- Spherical colony and comprised of 4,8,16 or 32 cells.
- Cells are arranged towards the periphery.
- Cup shaped chloroplast.
- Flagella absent.

Pediastrum

- Thallus multicellular and colonial.
- Colony disc shaped and stellate.
- 4 or more polygonal cells are present in the colony.
- Young cells are uninucleate, mature cells may contain 2 to 8 nuclei.
- Each cell contains a single, parietal and discoid chloroplast.

Ankistrodesmus

- Cells are solitary and lie in small loose groups, usually not enclosed in mucilaginous envelops.
- Cells are crescent shaped and slightly curved with both ends of the cells are tapering.
- A single chloroplast is present in each cell.

Closterium

- Cells are solitary, elongated without a median constriction.
- Each cell contains two sickle shaped chloroplasts with few pyrenoids.
- Cells appear to be divided into two semicells.

Cosmarium

- Thallus is unicellular, cells occur singly or in chains and are uninucleate.
- Each cell contain a single chloroplast.
- Each cell consist of two symmetrical halves connected with each other by a narrow bridge (isthmus) in which lies a single nucleus.

Filamentous algae

Spirogyra	*Ulothrix*	*Zygnema*	*Cladophora*	*Oedogonium*
Filaments unbranched and free floating	Filaments unbranched, long and free floating	Filaments unbranched and remain attached by means of a basal cell	Filaments branched	Filaments unbranched, float in masses
Cells almost as long as broad and in few species cells are longer than broad and each cell contains one central nucleus	Cells are broad and dark green, and contain one central nucleus	Cells long, cylindrical covered by mucilage, a single nucleus lies between the two chloroplasts	Cells long, walls stratified has a central vacoule, many nuclei lie on the periphery of each cell	Cells long, Cylindrical with fairly rigid walls, uninucleate and nucleus lie near the cell wall
Each cell has spiral, band/ ribbon shaped chloroplast and their number vary from one to several	Chloroplast band/ girdle shaped	Each cell has two stellate chloroplasts	Each cell has a single either reticulate or discoid chloroplast	Each cell has reticulate chloroplast
Chloroplast parietal in position and contain several pyrenoids	Chloroplast parietal in position and contain several pyrenoids	Chloroplast contain a single pyrenoid at the centre	Chloroplast is parietal in position and contain several pyrenoids	Chloroplast runs parallel to the cell axis and contain several pyrenoids

PLATE 1

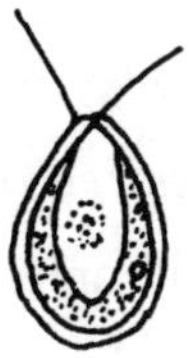

Chlamydomonas

Volvox

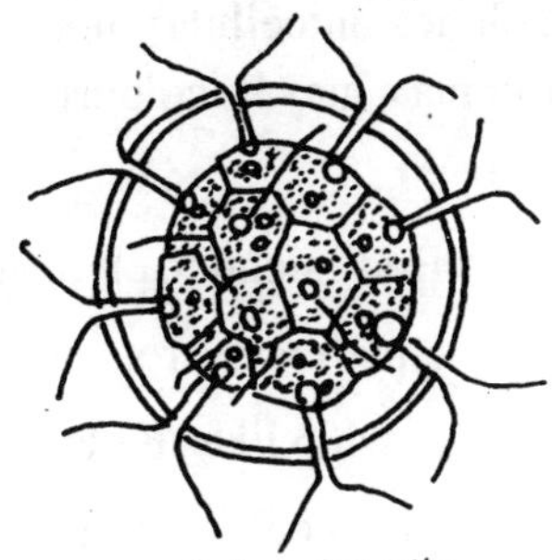

Sphaerocystis

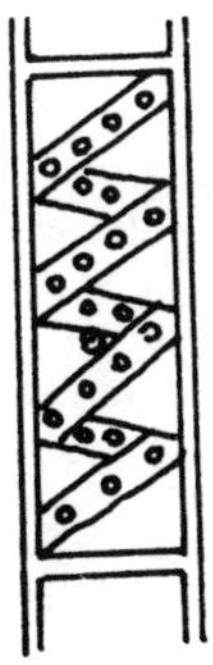

Spirogyra

Ulothrix

Zygnema

Cladophora

Oedogonium

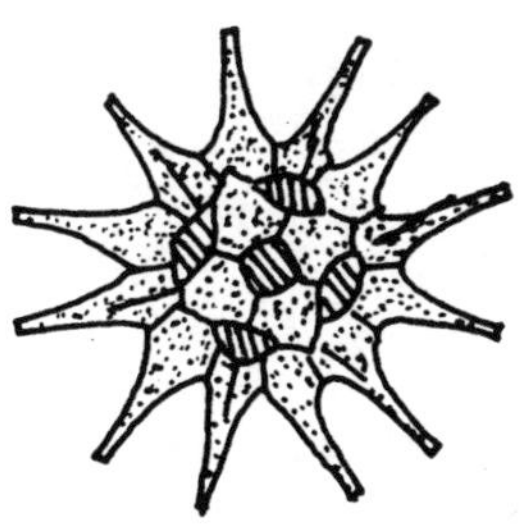

Pediastrum

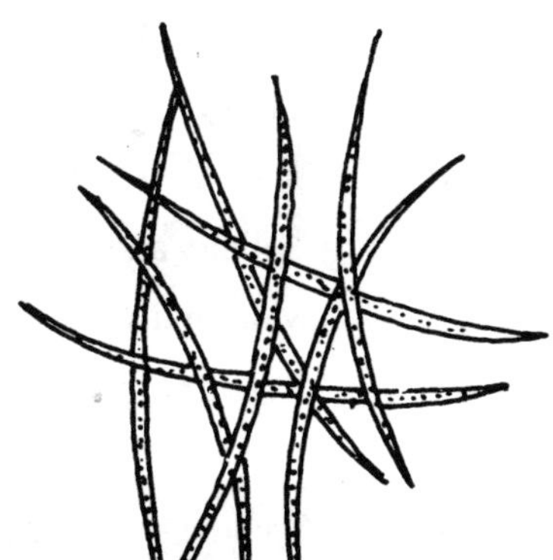

Ankistrodesmus

Closterium

Cosmarium

2. Euglenophyceae

It includes unicellular motile fresh water flagellates. Cells are solitary, not united in colonies. Protoplast may be colourless or with pigments as localized in green grass chloroplasts.

Euglena

- Body slender, elongated and spindle shaped.
- Anterior end rounded or blunt, middle part is broader and posterior end narrower.
- A whip like single flagellum, gullet and eye spot are seen at the anterior end.
- Many chloroplasts and a single nucleus is present in each organism.
- Contractile vacuole is also present.

Phacus

- A single flagellum arises from the anterior end.
- Bulb like cell with posterior end thread like.
- No gullet or eye spot.

3. Bacillariophyceae

- Members of this group are commonly known as diatoms.
- They may occur singly or in colonies.
- Cell wall is silicious which bears prominent markings.
- Some diatoms are circular in outline and some are elongated.
- Chloroplasts may be numerous or few.

Cyclotella

- Solitary and circular in outline.
- Marginal spines are absent.
- Area of prominent markings is limited to half of the circle.

Diatoma

- Spindle shaped with blunt ends.
- Markings are not much prominent.
- Many transverse septa are present.

Synedra

- Needle shaped cells are solitary or form fan like clusters.
- Cells are more longer than broad.
- Sometimes ends of the cells are slightly capitate.

Navicula

- Cells solitary, straight and symmetrical.

- Cells broader in the middle and narrower at both the ends and thus appear like a rolling pin
- Axial field is straight and clearly visible

4. Cyanophyceae (Blue green algae)

- Cells may lie singly or may form chains.
- Chains are enclosed in gelatinous sheath forming filaments.
- Definite nucleus is absent and instead a structure termed as centroplasm is present.
- In some species some cells develop thick walls and become spores known as heterocysts.
- Photosynthetic pigments include chlorophyll 'a', carotenes, xanthophylls-which impart blue green colour to algae,

Microcystis

- Colony spherical when young and appear net like when older.
- Pseudovacuoles often visible.

Spirulina

- Solitary cells are spirally coiled.
- Cell terminals round.
- Spirals not enclosed in a sheath.

Arthrospira

- Multicellular, unbranched filament without a sheath.
- Filament spirally coiled like Spirulina.

Oscillatoria

- Filaments straight, unbranched and solitary without a distinct sheath.
- Cells are discoidal and broad.
- Centroplasm, representing nucleus, occupies the centre, while chromatoplasm lines the periphery.

Nostoc

- Filaments contorted, colonial and enclosed in definite gelatinous sheath.
- Akinetes are arranged in chains.
- Towards the periphery cytoplasm include diffused pigments.
- Heterocysts (these are double walled and pale yellow coloured cells) are intercalary i.e., not terminal.

PLATE 2

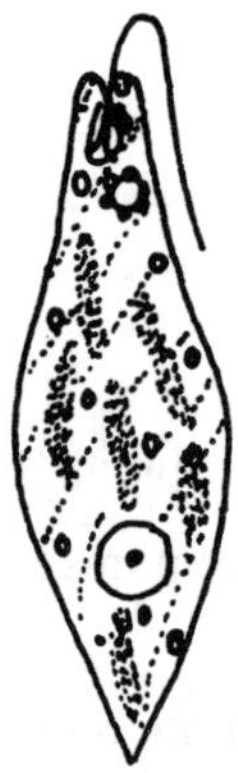

Euglena

Phacus

Cyclotella

Diatoma

Synedra

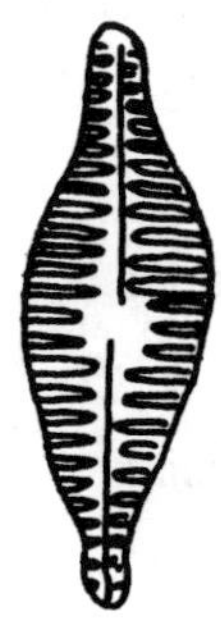

Navicula

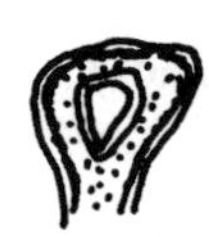

Microcystis

Nostoc

Spirulina

Arthrospira

Oscillatoria

Peridinium

Ceratium

5. Dinophyceae

- Unicellular flagellates with two terminal flagella.
- One of the flagellum is band shaped.
- Cells possess transverse and longitudinal furrows.

Peridinium

- Cell walls thick with distinct plates.
- Cells brownish and slightly flattened.
- A single thread like flagellum is present.

Ceratium

- Cells fusiform and with prominent projections.
- One of the projection is anterior and the other two or three are present on the posterior side.
- A single short flagellum is present.

ZOOPLANKTONS

The microscopic free swimming animal components of aquatic system constitutes zooplankton. They are mainly comprised of protozoa, rotifera, cladocera, copepoda and ostracoda.

1. Protozoa

- It includes unicellular organisms which may be uninucleate or multinucleate.
- Pseudopodia, cilia or flagella are present as locomotory organs.

Amoeba

- Unicellular, irregular in shape, uninucleate and with one contractile vacuole, food vacuoles are also seen.
- Pseudopodia are present.

Trinema

- Cells elongate to oval usually compressed.
- Uninucleate
- Body appear to be covered by circular or oval scales.

Paramoecium

- Unicellular, slipper shaped.
- Posterior end blunt, anterior pointed.
- Body covered by cilia.
- Two nuclei (micro and mega) and two contractile vacuoles are present.

2. Rotifera

Commonly called wheel animalcules

- Body bilaterally symmetrical, sac shaped, transparent and divided into a head, trunk and foot.
- A wheel like organ is present in the head region known as corona.
- Outer cuticular covering is flexible known as lorica.

Brachionus

- Lorica dorso-ventrally flattened.
- Simple eyes present. Number vary from one to three.
- Six anterior spines are visible. Foot opening posterior, long and worm like.
- End of foot is forked and thus two toes like structures are seen.

Keratella

- Lorica thick and dorsally curved, ventrally flattened or concave.
- 6 anterior spines are present in *Keratella cochlearis*, while in *K. tropica* in addition to 6 anterior spines, one long and one short spine on the posterior side are also seen.
- Foot and toes absent.

Rotaria

- Lorica dorso-ventrally flattened.
- Corona with two circles of cilia.
- Foot long, jointed and thin.
- Three toes are present.

3. Cladocera (Water fleas)

- A distinct head and trunk are present.
- Antennae and antennules are present in the head region.
- Head region also has a large compound eye and the smaller ocellus.
- Trunk region bears appendages and covered partly or completely by a bivalve carapace.

Daphnia

- Body compressed.
- Posterior part has sharp caudal spine.
- Head large and not very distinct from the body.
- A single eye and a small beak is present in the head region.
- Body surface covered by squarish markings.

PLATE 3

Amoeba

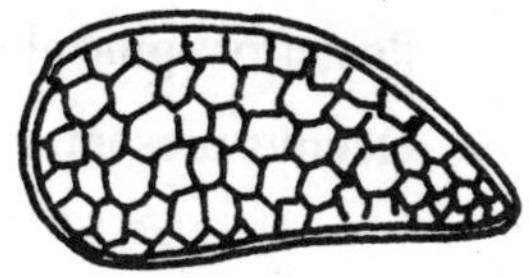

Trinema

Paramoecium

Brachionus

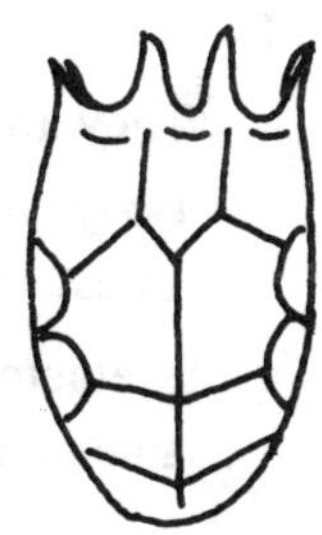

Keratella cochlearis

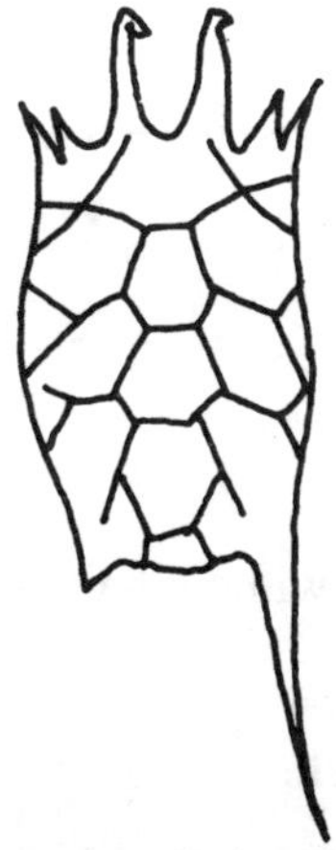

Keratella tropica

Rotaria

Ceriodaphnia

- Head small depressed and distinctly marked from the trunk region.
- Beak is absent.
- Valves of the body are round with hexagonal markings.
- Posterior spine absent.
- Ocellus present.

Moina

- Head large and thick, rounded in front and bent downwards.
- Beak is absent.
- Posterior spine is absent, valves elliptical with minute spines on the ventral side.
- Ocellus (eye) present.

4. Copepoda

- They are small crustaceans.
- Body is divided into two regions by distinct articulations-anterior metasome and a posterior urosome.
- Metastome is divided into Head and thorax. Head bears antennae and antennules.
- Urosome includes the last 1 or 2 thoracic segments and abdomen.

Cyclops

- Metasome broader than urosome.
- Antennae are shorter and with spines.
- 2 egg sacs are seen on either side of the thoracic region in case of female cyclops.
- Caudal part has longitudinal dorsal ridge and inner margin armed with fine hairs.

Diaptomus

- Slender body.
- Metasome larger, broader than urosome.
- Antennae long without spines.
- Caudal part has short furcal processes without hairs or spines.

5. Ostracoda (Seed shrimps or mussel shrimps)

- Entire body is enclosed in a bivalve shell.
- Antennae large situated at anterior end.
- Body is not distinctly segmented with caudal furca.

PLATE 4

Daphnia

Ceriodaphnia

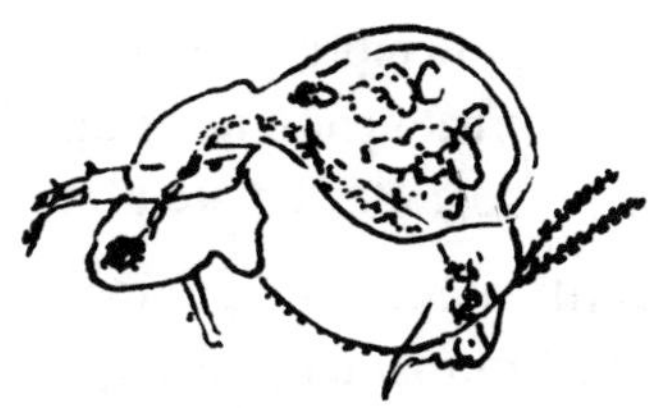

Moina

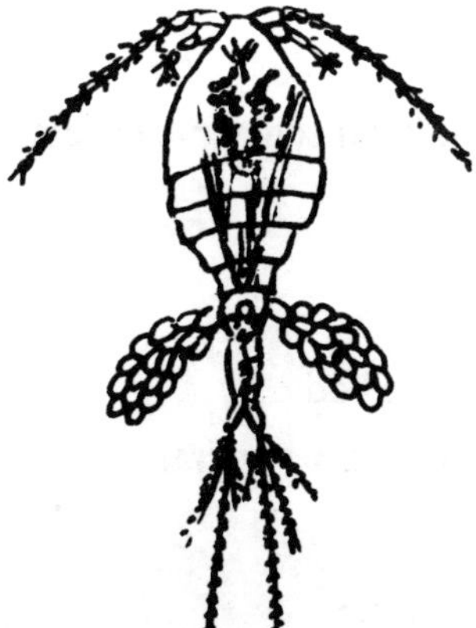

Cyclops

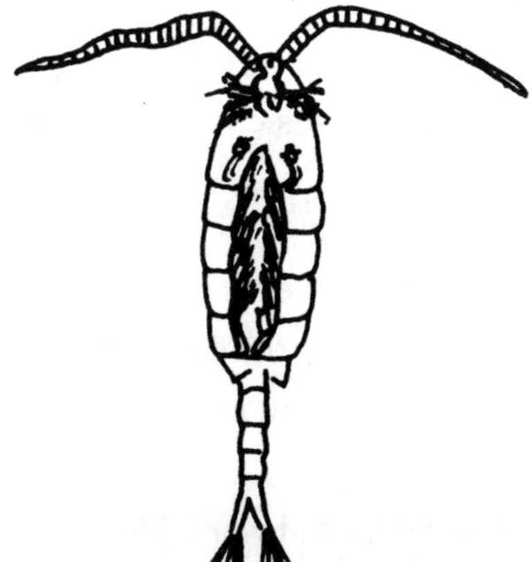

Diaptomus

Cypris

Cypris

- Shells broad, length lesser than twice the width.
- Bivalve shell covered with hair.
- Left half is larger than the right half.

BIOLOGICAL CHARACTERISTICS OF POND SEDIMENT

Collection and preservation of sediment samples

Take a known volume of the sediment and wash through a set of sieves (mesh size 2.0 mm followed by 0.5mm). Collect macro and microorganisms with the help of a pair of forceps and preserve in 70% alcohol or 4% formaline. Those benthos which escape sieving process may be collected as follows :

Add more water to the residual sediment and add to it 5g of sucrose. With this treatment remaining benthos will float on the surface. The benthic organisms so collected are also preserved as described above.

Identify important groups of benthic fauna which generally belong to Annelida (oligochaeta), Arthropoda (insecta) and Mollusca (gastropoda and bivalvia).

Calculations

$$\text{Benthos/m}^2 = \frac{\text{Average No. of organisms per sample}}{\text{Area of the sample (cm}^2\text{)}} \times 100 \times 100 \text{ or } 10^4$$

IDENTIFICATION OF COMMON BENTHOS (See plate 5)

1. Oligochaeta

- It includes segmented worms. The body is long cylindrical and metamerically segmented.
- Head is indistinct and tentacles are absent.
- Parapodia absent, setae few in number and present in all segments except the first.

Dero

- Head is distinct and eyes absent.
- Setae are present on the dorsal and ventral side of the body.
- Posterior end modified into a cliliated gill bearing retractile respiratory organ.

Chaetogaster

- Body transparent and worm like.
- Head is distinct with anterior end broader.
- Setae present only on the ventral side.

Branchiura

- Body reddish and contractile. Head not distinct.
- Anterior segments are smaller.
- Posterior segments of the body bears a dorsal and a ventral gill, however, the gills are absent from the last segment.

Tubifex

- Body reddish.
- Prostomium short and triangular.
- Body coils into a ball with slight disturbance.
- Segments clearly demarcated.

2. Diptera

- This order of class Insecta includes common flies, the adults of which are never truly aquatic, however, their larvae are aquatic and form a bulk of the benthic fauna.
- They are without jointed thoracic legs, with abdominal prolegs or entirely legless.

Chaborus

- Body is long and transparent.
- Thoracic segments are fused, enlarged and distinct.
- Last abdominal segment with a stiff comb of hair on the ventral side.
- Gill like appendages are present at the tip of the abdomen.

Chironomous

- Pinkish red in colour.
- Antenna five segmented and short.
- Abdomen without bristles.
- Paired pseudopods on the anal end.

Tanypus

- Body long, slightly broader near the front end and tapering behind.
- Antennae elongated.
- A pair of false thoracic legs are present, which are fused near their base.

3. Mollusca

- This group includes animals with soft unsegmented coelomate bodies covered with shells.
- Body is divided into head, visceral mass, mantle and a foot.
- Shell may be univalve (snails) or bivalve (clams).

PLATE 5

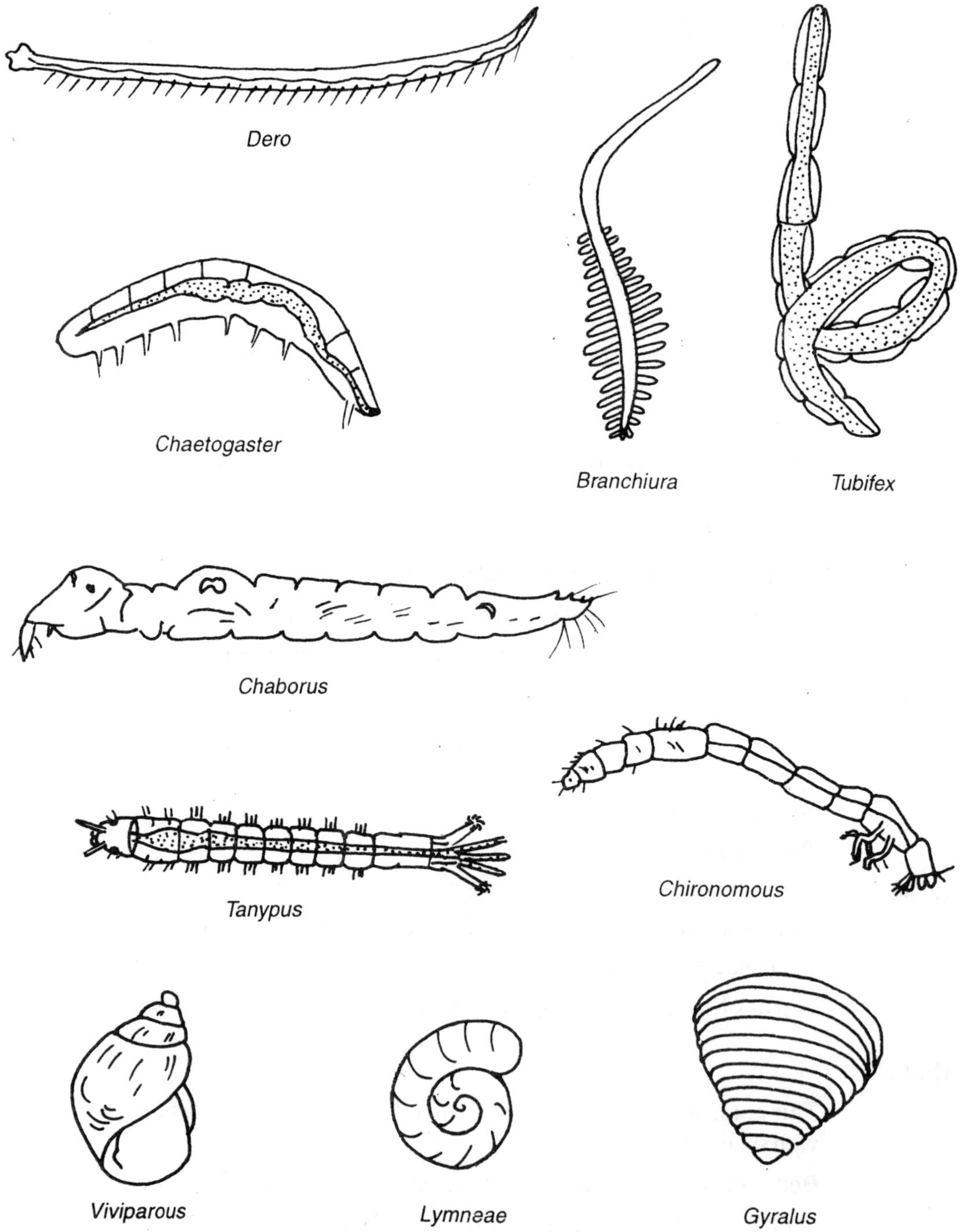
Dero
Chaetogaster
Branchiura
Tubifex
Chaborus
Chironomous
Tanypus
Viviparous
Lymneae
Gyralus

Viviparous

- Shell univalve and thin, globose and whorls convex.
- A small foot is present.
- Operculum with simple outer margin.

Lymnaea

- Shell thin and imperforate.
- Shell spire dextral (to right).
- One pair of flattened tentacles with eyes at their base.

Gyralus

- Shell discoid and small in size.
- Whorls of shell are few in number and in the same general plane.

EXERCISES

Exercise 1 : Calculate species diversity (d) from the following data by Margelf's diversity index and compare it with Shannon and Weaver's diversity index

a) *Phytoplankton*

Pediastrum, 400; *Spirogyra*, 1300; *Cosmarium*, 840; *Crucigenia*, 520; *Navicula*, 200; *Synedra*, 640; *Nitzschia*, 330; *Cymbella*, 480; *Microcystis*, 280; *Nostoc*, 160; Total population of phytoplankton = 5500

Number of species = 10 ($\bar{d}$=2.40, 2.92)

b) *Zooplankton*

Keratella, 200; *Brachionvs*, 80; *Cyclops*, 200; *Daphnia*, 400; *Diaphanosoma*, 100; *Chydorous*, 160; *Bosmina*, 80; *Cypris*, 40. Total number of zooplankton = 1260

Number of species = 8 ($\bar{d}$=2.26, 3.31)

Exercise 2 : Diurnal changes in DO concentrations are given. Calculate net primary productivity.

S.No.	Time	DO (mg l^{-1})		Productivity
1.	0800	3.7±0.18		
			$\frac{5.7-3.7}{4}$	= 0.5mg $O_2 l^{-1}$ hr^{-1}
2.	1200	5.7±0.18		
			$\frac{5.7-4.9}{4}$	= 0.2 mg O_2 l^{-1} hr^{-1}
3.	1600	4.9±0.18		
			$\frac{4.9-2.4}{4}$	= 0.63 mg O_2 l^{-1} hr^{-1}
4.	2000	2.4±0.0		

Mean productivity (mg O_2 l^{-1} h^{-1}) $= 0.5+0.2+0.63 = \frac{1.33}{3} = 0.44$

Mean productivity mg O_2 l^{-1} h^{-1} = 0.44±0.18 mg O_2 l^{-1} h^{-1}

Net primary productivity mg C l^{-1} h^{-1} = 0.44 × 0.375 = 0.165

Where,

0.375 is the factor for converting O_2 values to C values (see experiment 1.38a)

Exercise 3 : Collect water samples, identify and prepare whole mounts of both phytoplankton and zooplankton.

CHAPTER 2

Pond Management Practices

Experiment 2.1: *Describe the construction and management of a fish farm.*

Introduction and visit to a fish farm

For commercialization of fish culture operations, a fish culturist needs specific types of ponds for the culture of particular fish/shellfish species and their life history stages. These ponds are known as nursery, rearing and stocking ponds, which collectively constitute a fish farm. Great care needs to be exercised while selecting the best possible site for the fish farm and pond construction. The success in fish production largely depends on a suitable site/topography of the fish farm.

Approximate area of a fish farm

Area = about 2.5 to 10 ha.

Examine the following characteristics for a typical/suitable/successful fish farm.

Topography

It should be a gently sloping area and the basin be surrounded on three sides by high land with a narrow outlet on the fourth side. The terrain should be non-rocky with atleast 2m deep soil.

Soil type

It should be free from seepage (i.e., vertical and horizontal seepage). A soil containing 10% clay, 20% silt and 70% sand is considered to be ideal for pond construction. Heavy soils, such as clay, silty-clay and clay-loam should be the first choice.

For easy field testing of the soil, prepare a tight ball of the moist soil, if it does not crumble on throwing/handling/squeezing, it may be regarded as satisfactory.

Water supply

A perennial source of water supply with good physico-chemical characteristics are required for a successful fish farm.

Power supply

Power supply is another necessity at a good fish farm for carryingout various day to day operations (Lighting, tube-well running,water transfer, water analysis etc.).

Site

Site should be easily approachable , so that one can easily go for disposing of their products to the market and also transport spawn/seed etc.

Types of ponds

Ponds can be classified on the basis of their utilization, such as nursery ponds, rearing ponds and stocking ponds. A fourth type of ponds are also constructed for broodstock management/breeding and spawning etc.

Nursery ponds : These are shallow and small ponds used for spawn rearing upto advance fingerling stage (i.e. upto 50 mm). Its area ranges from 0.04-0.05 ha and size may vary from 25m×16m, or 20m×20m or 25m × 20m, and depth from 0.5-1.5m.

Rearing ponds :These ponds are used for rearing fry (25mm) or advance fingerlings to grow to about 150mm. These ponds are larger than nursery ponds and smaller than stocking ponds. Their area varies from 0.08-0.1 ha and the depth range from 1.5-2.0m. The convenient size may vary from 40m×20m or 50m×20m.

Stocking ponds : These are mostly perennial ponds and are used for rearing fingerlings to table sized or marketable size fish i.e. upto 500-750g. Area of these ponds varies from 0.2 to 2.0 ha and the water depth ranges from 2.0 to 3.5m.

Preparation and management of different types of ponds

Management of nursery ponds

Follow the following management practices for the preparation of nursery ponds :

(A) *Pre-stocking management practices*

1. Eradicate the weeds manually or by dewatering the ponds.
2. Eradicate the predatory fishes using mahua oil cake.
3. Lime the nursery ponds, 15 days prior to fertilization.
4. Fertilize the ponds using organic wastes-farm yard manure, cow-dung, poultry waste etc. or inorganic fertilizers (SSP, urea). (See tables 4-5).
5. Eradicate the aquatic insects; 24h prior to stocking.

Note : *Bottle green colour of the pond water is indicative of productive waters.*

(B) *Stocking management practices*

6. Stock the spawn preferably during morning or evening hours i.e. when the water temperature is low.

(C) *Post-stocking management practices*

7. Follow supplementary feeding schedules immediately or within 1-2 days of stocking.

8. Feed the spawn with a mixture of oilcake and ricebran (1:1 ratio by weight) or mixture of fishmeal, silk worm pupae and oilcake in equal ratio. For first five days, feed be given @ four times the initial weight of the spawn, and then for the following five days give feed @ 8 times the initial weight of the spawn.
9. The spawn be harvested at the end of 12 days of stocking, i.e. the fry (20-25 mm) be transferred to rearing ponds.

Management of rearing and stocking ponds

Follow the following management practices before stocking :

(A) *Prestocking management practices*

1. Eradicate the weeds.
2. Dug the surface of pond bottom before the application of fertilizers and wait for 15-20 days for complete drying.
3. Broadcast lime.
4. Wait for 7 days and broadcast the first dose of manure/fertilizers (See tables 4-5).
5. Let a little water flow in the ponds and wait for another 7-15 days.
6. Fill the ponds with water and apply the second dose of manure/fertilizer.
7. Wait for another 15 days for the development of natural fish food organisms, when the colour of water becomes bottle green.

(B) *Stocking management practices*

8. Stock the fry/fingerlings (See table 6).

(C) *Post-stocking management practices*

9. Feed the fish @ 2-3% of their body weight.
10. Sample the fish periodically to adjust the weight of the feed and for monitoring the health.
11. Transfer the fish when about 110-150 mm (about 3 months period) to stocking ponds.

Management practices for successful fish culture

Efficient pond fish culture entails special preparation to receive spawn, fry or fingerlings. The steps commonly adapted towards preparation of ponds includes (a) Eradication of weeds/ macrophtyes (b) eradication of predatory and weed fishes (c) Lime application (d) Fertilization and their rate of application (e) Eradication of predatory insects and other predators (f) Stocking density and ratio (g) Control of parasites and diseases (h) Supplementary feeds.

(a) Eradication of weed plants/macrophytes/algal blooms

Weeds and grasses create difficulty during the harvesting of the fry and consume the pond nutrients and provide shelter to harmful insects.

Aquatic weeds can be kept in check by using the following methods :

(i) *Manual method* :

This is the best and cheapest method in case of small shallow units.

- Periodically remove aquatic plants by handpicking/uprooting.
- Dry and burn the collected weeds.

(ii) *Mechanical method*

Materials

- Dragging log weeders fitted with spikes and barbed wire.

OR

- Long handled forks and sickles.

Procedure

Mechanical method is adapted in smaller or larger ponds especially for tough and firmly rooted plants.

- Remove rooted submerged weeds by dragging log weeders fitted with spikes and barbed wire or cut them with long handled forks and sickles.
- The weeds must be cut at least, 30cm under water surface.
- Dry and burn them.

(iii) *Chemical method*

Control of weeds by chemical means has one advantage that it ploughs the nutrients taken away by the weeds back into the pond by killing the weeds *in situ*.

Materials

- Sprayer
- Weedicides e.g. (a) 2,4-dichlorophenoxy acetic acid, (b) Taficide 80 (2,4-D sodium salt 80%) (c) Surf. (d) Sodium arsenite (e) Simazine

Procedure

- For eradication of marginal weeds prepare 3-4% solution of 2,4-D sodium salt alongwith 0-25% surf. Spray it on weeds especially on foliar region.
- For emergent weeds like lily, spray 2,4-D salt at 1.5% concentration along with 0.25-1% detergent (surf). For weeds like Nymphea, spread copper sulphate with mud on the bottom soil in 4-5 intermittent doses, totalling 175 kg/ha.

Submerged weeds can be chemically controlled as follows :

(a) Anhydrous ammonia @ 225 kg/hectare can effectively control submerged weeds.

(b) Simazine (5 ppm) is also effective weedicde for controlling submerged weeds.

(c) Paraquat @ 2 ppm is also effective.

- Algal blooms can be controlled by spraying simazine at a small dose of 0.5-1.0 ppm

(iv) *Biological control*

Biological control involves the control of weeds by providing some exotic agents such as insects, snails or fishes.

- Algal blooms could be checked by providing a thick cover of duck weeds (e.g. *Lemna, Pistia, Salvinia* so that sunlight could be cutoff to hamper their normal life processes and thereby bringing about their kill.
- Filamentous algae, rooted or unrooted submerged weeds and duck weeds can be controlled by employing certain species of fish as biological control agents. Common carp, gourami, tilapia and grass carp are well known weed eating fish. Tilapia and common carp take filamentous algae and grass carp feeds voraciously on *Hydrilla, Vallisneria, Najas, Potamogeton* and duckweeds.

In the absence of above mentioned weeds, grass carp can also feed on *Ceratophyllum, Myriophyllum, Nechamandra, Limnophila, Nitella, Elodea, Hydrocharis, Phragmites* and *Typha* as a second choice. In a day, grass carp feeds more than its body weight of preferred aquatic weeds. Weeds like *Hydrilla, Vallisneria* and *Potamogeton* in a 1 ha pond can be controlled by introducing 250-300 grass carp each weighing between 0.5 to 1.0 kg.

Predators like crabs, frogs and tadpoles can also be removed by repeated nettings before stocking the spawn/fry.

(b) Eradication of predatory and weed fishes

A large number of predatory (sal, magur, singhi, pangas, tengara, boal, pabda, koi, nandus, kuchia, cheetal, belay, bam etc.) and weed fishes (such as Puntius, chela, chanda, lowrala, colisa, dankoni, labuka and daurika etc.) are found to occur in ponds. Predatory fishes feed on spawn resulting in a heavy loss. Moreover, these fishes compete for feed, space and oxygen with the fry. It is, therefore, essential to eradicate these fishes from the nursery ponds.

Methods of eradication

1. Dewatering

Nursery ponds are dewatered, predatory and weed fishes are identified and removed.

2. Manual method

It includes repeated nettings in order to remove the weed fishes.

3. By the application of fish poisons/piscicides

Fish poisons such as bleaching powder, seed powder of *Barringtonia acutangula*, are used to eradicate predatory fishes. Various fish poisons and rates of their application are given below :

(i)	*Barringtonia acutangula* (Seed powder)	@ 150 kg/ha/month (Toxicity 5 days)
(ii)	*Croton tiglium* (Seed powder)	@ 40-50 kg/ha/month (Toxicity 5 days)
(iii)	*Millettia piscidia* (Root powder)	@ 40-50 kg/ha/month (Toxicity 5 days)
(iv)	*Bassia latifolia* (Mahua oil cake)	@ 2500 kg/ha/month (Toxicity upto 12-15 days)
(v)	Bleaching powder	@ 350 kg/ha/month (Toxicity upto 7-8 days)
(vi)	Bleaching powder + Urea	@ 175 kg/ha/month @ 100 kg/ha/month

Note : Do not use piscicides in nursery ponds

(c) Lime application

Application of lime depends upon the pH of the pond sediment and water. It is essentially required when the soil water reaction is acidic and is usually applied @ 200 kg-400 kg ha^{-1} y^{-1}. If soil pH is below 6.5, lime may be applied @ 300-500 kg $ha^{-1}y^{-1}$. Lime application may be done at least 7-15 days prior to the application of fertilizers.

(d) Fertilization and their rate of application

Fertilizers are used to enhance pond productivity by providing nutrients. They are mainly of two types :

1. Organic
2. Inorganic

Organic manures

They are composite in nature and are chiefly obtained from animal wastes (such as cowdung, poultry, piggery or cattle wastes etc.), plant or vegetal detritus.

The dosage of organic fertilizers for fish ponds chiefly depends on their origin, nutrient status of pond water/sediment.

Rate of application of commonly used organic manures in fish culture ponds are given in table 4.

TABLE 4

Livestock wastes	Rate of application
Cow-dung	@ 10000-20000 kg $ha^{-1} y^{-1}$
Poultry	@ 3000-5000 kg $ha^{-1} y^{-1}$
Pig manure	@ 4000-5000 kg $ha^{-1} y^{-1}$
Duck waste	@ 4000-5000 kg $ha^{-1} y^{-1}$

Inorganic fertilizers

Major nutrients which are supplied to fish ponds are nitrogen, phosphorus, potassium and calcium. These are supplied in the form of urea $CO(NH_2)_2$ superphosphates (Single Super Phosphate-SSP; and Triple superphosphate-TSP) and potash. Sometimes manganous sulphate ($MnSO_4$) is also used to enhance zooplankton production (Table 5).

TABLE 5

Fertilizer	Recommended rate of application
N (Nitrogen fertilizer)	5 to 10 kg ha^{-1} $(2\ wks)^{-1}$
Phosphates	8.75 to 17.5 kg P_2O_5 ha^{-1} $(2\ wks)^{-1}$
$MnSO_4$	1 kg ha^{-1}
K (Potash)	40 kg $ha^{-1} y^{-1}$ (in three split doses, if required)

Potassium is mostly not a limiting factor, however, if needed it is supplied as K_2O.

Note : *Manures/fertilizers are invariably dissolved in water before application*

(e) Eradication of predatory insects and other predators

A large number of aquatic insects, such as water beetles, aquatic bugs, water scorpion, water stick insect, dragon fly nymphs etc. are present in the ponds which devour spawn/fry voraciously and needs to be controlled. The general and effective method for their eradication is the application of oil-soap emulsion which is prepared as follows :

Principle

Since insects are air breathers, therefore, application of oil-soap emulsion will kill most of the insects by choking their spiracles.

Preparation of oil soap emulsion

(Cheap soap @ 18 kg + Vegetable oil 56 kg) ha^{-1}

OR

- (Teepol-B-300-560 ml + Vegetable oil 56 kg) ha^{-1}

OR

- (Teepol-B-300-560 ml + Kerosine 75 l) ha^{-1}

OR

- (Teepol-B-300-560 ml + light speed Diesel 50 l) ha^{-1}

Mix the ingredients and shake vigrously before use as follows :

Spray the emulsion on pond water surface one day prior to stocking of spawn/fry.

Precautions

- Apply the emulsion on windless days.
- Do not use oil-soap emulsion in nursery ponds.

(f) Stocking density and ratio

Table 6. Approximate stocking denstiy in different types of ponds

Sr.No.	Name of the pond	Stocking density
1.	Nursery ponds	0.2-10 millions ha^{-1}
2.	Rearing ponds	Upto 20,000 $(0.1\ ha)^{-1}$
3.	Stocking ponds	4000-10,000 fingerlings ha^{-1}

Species ratio in rearing and stocking ponds

Following spcies ratio may be kept in mind before stocking in rearing and stocking ponds :

(i) Catla : Rohu : Mrigal

3 : 4 : 3

OR

4 : 3 : 3

(ii) Catla : Rohu : Mrigal : Common carp

3 : 4 : 1 : 2

(iii) Silver carp : Grass carp : Common carp

4 : 3 : 3

Composite fish culture (Six species combination)

Following percentage of the species be selected :

(i) Surface feeder - like Catla, silver carp 30%

(ii)	Column feeder	-	like Rohu 15%
(iii)	Bottom feeder	-	like Mrigal, Calbasu/common carp 40%
(iv)	Macrovegetation feeder	-	like grass carp 5-15%.

(It depends on the availability of aquatic weeds in ponds).

Four species culture combination

(i)	Catla :	Rohu :	Mrigal :	Common carp
	30-40%	20-30%	10-15%	20-25%

Three species culture combinantion

Catla :	Rohu :	Mrigal
40%	30%	30%

(g) Control of parasites and diseases

Random netting, monitoring and care should be taken to prevent any deterioration in the physico-chemical condition of the pond soil and water.

(h) (i) Supplementary feeds

Natural fish feed in the pond is normally not sufficient, therefore, supplementary feed be given in the ponds for proper and higher growth. Supplementary feed items are given depending upon their availability in a particular area. The commonly used supplementary feeds for the Indian major carp are : oilcakes (groundnut, coconut, mustard oil cake) or rice bran (deoiled) and a variety of leguminous seeds. The other supplementary feeds which are of animal origin includes fishmeal, prawnmeal, clam meal, slaughter house waste, blood meal, meat meal, poultry waste and silk worm pupae etc.

(ii) Rate of feeding

In this region normally a mixture of rice bran and oilcake (1:1) mixed in equal proportions is given to the fish @ 2-3% of their body weight. Carp spawn/fry needs large number of natural food organisms and being very tender can feed only on small zooplankters. Follow the following schedule for giving supplementary feed :

1. 2-5 days after stocking - equal to four times the weight of the spawn.
2. 6-10 days after stocking - eight times the initial weight of the spawn stocked.
3. Feed the fry @ 3% during the first month @ 4% during second month and @ 5% during the third month.
4. Depending upon the natural feed available in ponds, feed the fingerlings and adults @ 3-4% of body weight.

How to feed the baby fish or an adult

1. To soften the feed, soak it in water overnight. Add the semi-solid food in nursery ponds. Same procedure can be followed for feeding the adult fish.

2. Bamboo baskets are also hanged in the ponds, containing overnight soaked food.

3. Soak the food overnight in water, make balls and place the balls at convenient and fixed places in the ponds every day or on alternate days depending upon the feeding schedule is being followed.

4. Gunny bags with holes at the bottom containing food are also hanged in the ponds for feeding the fish.

Exercise 1 : Calculate the quantity of piscicides required for treatment of a pond/water body

Accurate quanity of piscicides required can be calculated as follows :

(i) Quantity (kg) of piscicide powder/cake = $L \times W \times D \times Dose$ required in rectangular and square ponds

Where,

L = Length of rectangular pond

W = Width of the rectangular pond

D = Depth of the rectangular pond

Dose = Recommended dose in kg/ha/month

(ii) Quantity (kg) of cake, powder required (in kg) for circular ponds = $R^2 \times 3.143 \times D \times Dose$

Where,

R = Radius of the pond in m

D = Depth of pond in m

Dose = Recommended dose in kg/ha/month

Exercise 2 : Calculate the quantity of earth required for making a bundh of a given pond.

Area of pond	=	2000 m^2 (50×40m)
Total length	=	50+40+50+40 = 180m
Crown width	=	1 m
Dry side slope	=	1:1
Wet side slope	=	1:1:1.5
Bundh height	=	1 m

Earth required for one meter long bundh

$$= \frac{1 \times 1 \times 1.5}{2} + (1 \times 1 \times 1) + \frac{1 \times 1 \times 1}{2} = 2.25\ m^3$$

Total earth required for 180 m long bundh

= **$180 \times 2.25 m^3 = 405\ m^3$**

Exercise 3 : Find out the number of fish seed to be transported in a given volume of water

Where the volume of water is 15L

Oxygen contents = 8 mg l^{-1}

Weight of individual fry = 1 mg

Period of transport = 8 h

Rate of oxygen consumption = 200 mg/kg/h

$$N = \frac{(DO-2) \times V}{C \times h}$$

$$N = \frac{(8-2) \times 15}{0.2 \times 8} = \frac{6 \times 15}{0.2 \times 8} = \frac{90}{1.6} = 56.25$$

DO = Dissolved oxygen contents in water mg l^{-1}

V = Total volume of water (L^{-1})

C = Rate of oxygen consumption by individual (mg kg^{-1} h^{-1})

h = Period of transport in hours

Exercise 4 : Ask students to write a field report of their visit to the fish farm.

Identification of weeds (See plates 6-7)

Table 7 summarizes the important groups of weeds generally found in fish ponds. These can be identified using suitable keys and monographs.

Table 7 : Aquatic weeds

	Groups	Common examples
(i)	Floating weeds (weeds which have their leaves freely floating on the surface of water and roots hanging underneath)	*Eichhornia, Pistia, Lemna, Azolla, Wolffia*
(ii)	Marginal weeds (weeds growing along the shore line of the ponds)	*Typha, Colocasia, Ipomoea, Sagittaria, Jussiaea, Marsilea*
(iii)	Emergent weeds (plants that are rooted at the bottom but emerge out of water)	*Nymphaea, Trapa*
(iv)	Submerged weeds (plants that always remain sub-merged under water)	*Hydrilla, Vallisneria, Potamogetom, Ceratophyllum, Myriophyllum*
(v)	Filamentous algae (Algae that are scattered in the water body)	*Microcystis, Oscillatoria, Anabaena*

PLATE 6

Eichhornia

Lemna

Azolla

Wolffia

Ipomoea

Jussiaea

Marsilea

PLATE 7

Nymphaea

Trapa

Hydrilla

Potamogeton

Vallisneria

Ceratophyllum

Myriophyllum

Identification of predatory Insects (See plate 8)

1. ***Notonecta*** (Back swimmer)
   - (i) Very harmful to the fry and spawn, could be dried and used as fish feed.
   - (ii) Body elongated.
   - (iii) Head is inserted in thorax, antennae shorter than thorax.
   - (iv) Legs dissimilar and longer.
   - (v) Dorsal side brown and ventrally whitish.
   - (vi) Front appendages with distinct claw like structure.

2. ***Belostoma*** (Giant water bug)
   - (i) Antennae shorter than head
   - (ii) One pair of large stalked eyes
   - (iii) Appendages flat and compressed with distinct claws
   - (iv) The first pair of legs are broad in front like the pedipalps of a scorpion

3. ***Ranatra***
   - (i) Long stick like appearance
   - (ii) Prothorax narrower than head
   - (iii) Size 0.5" to 3" long
   - (iv) Legs long and cylindrical, anterior legs longer than posterior legs
   - (v) Two breathing tubes at the posterior end of the abdomen are present.

4. ***Gerris***
   - (i) Rust brown in colour
   - (ii) First segment of antennae longer than the second and third
   - (iii) First thoracic segment is more long than broad
   - (iv) Wings are absent
   - (v) First pair of legs is prehensile

5. ***Nepa*** (water-scorpion)
   - (i) Broad, oval and flat body
   - (ii) Prothorax broader than head
   - (iii) Wings are present
   - (iv) Forelegs are broad in front and are like the pedipalps of a scorpion (prehensile)
   - (v) Breathing tube is in the shape of a spine

PLATE 8

Back swimmer (*Notonecta*)

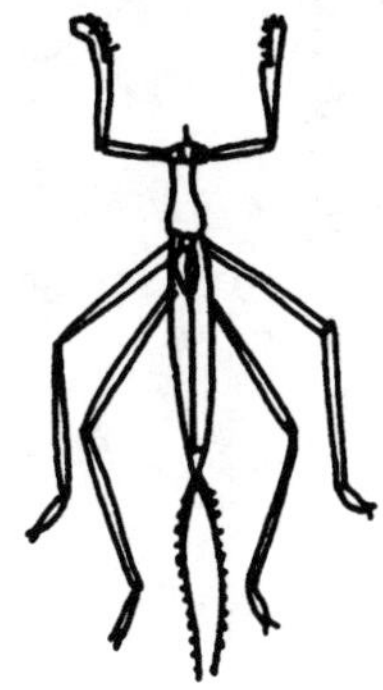

Water stick insect (*Ranatra*)

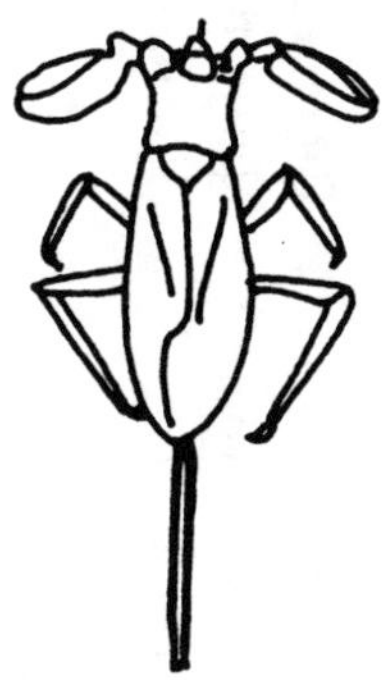

Water scorpion

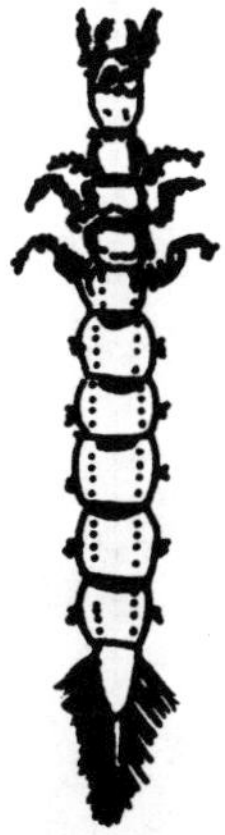

Cybister larva

Dragon fly numph

Table 8 : Summary of fish farm management practices

	Nursery ponds	Rearing ponds	Stocking ponds
1. Type	Seasonal	Seasonal/perennial	Seasonal/perennial
2. Area (ha)	0.04-0.05	0.08-0.1	0.2-2.0
3. Convenient size	25×16m/25×20m/20×20m	40×20m/50×20m	80'×20' - 300'×80'
4. Approximate depth (m)	1.0	1.5-2.0	2.0-3.5
5. Approximate No. of ponds in an ideal fish farm	4	12	6
6. Stocking rate	0.2-10 millions ha^{-1}	About 20,000 ha^{-1}	4000-10000 fingerling ha^{-1}
7. Method of eradication of weeds	Manual	Manual or Biological control	Manual, biological or chemical control
8. Eradication of weed/ predatory fishes	By repeated netting and use of HIJAL seed powder @ 150kg ha^{-1} $month^{-1}$ OR Croton seed powder @ 40-50 kg ha^{-1} $month^{-1}$ OR Bishloti root powder @ 40-50 kg ha^{-1} $month^{-1}$ OR Mahua oilcake @ 2500 kg ha^{-1} $month^{-1}$	By repeated netting and application of piscicides (like mahua oil cake)	By application of mahua oil cake

Table 9 : Identification of Indian major carp fry

	Mrigal	Catla	Rohu
1. **Head and body**	Head small, body slender	Head large, dorsal profile convex, ventral concave	Medium size head
2. **Barbels**	Barbels absent	Barbels absent	A pair of whitish or light greyish maxillary barbels are present
3. **Caudal peduncle spot**	More or less trinangular dark spot at the caudal peduncle	No distinct spot	A diffused transverse band present at the caudal peduncle
4. **Lips**	Thin	Thick	Fringed
5. **Caudal fin and others**	Lower lobe of caudal fin has a reddish tinge	Margins of the dorsal and caudal fin are darker, first ray of the dorsal fin is black	No distinct features
6. **Operculum**	No special feature	Opercular region bright red	No special feature

6. ***Cybister*** (Diving bettle)

(i) Streamlined body

(ii) Carnivorous with biting mouth parts

(iii) Adults are strong swimmers with legs modified for swimming

(iv) Gills are present at the sides of the abdomen

7. ***Dystiscus***

(i) Head flat with piercing jaws

(ii) Body partly segmented and pointed at both the ends

(iii) Breathing tube located at the end of the abdomen

Identification of fingerlings of culturable fish species

1. ***Catla catla***

(i) Head broad

(ii) No Barbels

(iii) Dorsal profile and ventral profile concave

(iv) Lips thick and not fringed

(v) Mouth upturned

(vi) No distinct spot on the body or at the caudal peduncle

(vii) Dorsal, caudal and anal fins dark greyish in colour

(viii) Opercular region brightly reddish

2. ***Labeo rohita***

(i) A pair of light or white maxillary barbels

(ii) Lips fringed and thick

(iii) Mouth inferior

(iv) A dark diffused vertical band present at caudal peduncle

3. ***Cirrhinus mrigala***

(i) Lips thin and non-fringed

(ii) Terminal mouth

(iii) More or less triangular diamond shaped dark spot on the caudal peduncle

(iv) Tip of the lower lobe of the caudal fin has a reddish tinge in longer sized fry

(v) Scales on the body are shining yellow

4. ***Labeo calbasu***

(i) Lips thick and fringed

(ii) Two pairs of thick barbels present

(iii) The early fry is dark black in colour

(iv) The lips of fins are black and black colour gradually diffuses on the lower part of fins

(v) Yellow and dark bands present throughout the body of the fingerlings

5. *Cyprinus carpio* (var. communis, nudus and specularis)

(i0 Body oblong

(ii) Snout rounded

(iii) Mouth inferior with two pairs of barbels

(iv) Dorsal fin opposite to ventral fin

6. Silver carp (*Hypothalmichthys molitrix*)

(i) Body oblong

(ii) Slightly compressed body covered with small scales

(iii) Head pointed

(iv) Snout bluntly rounded

(v) Abdomen keeled

(vi) Origin of dorsal fin behind ventral

(vii) Body shining, silver coloured

7. Grass carp *(Ctenopharyngodan idella)*

(i) Body elongated and compressed

(ii) Head broad and short

(iii) Snout rounded

(iv) No barbels

(v) Mouth subterminal and rounded

CHAPTER 3

Fishing Gears

Experiment 3.1 : *Identification of different types of fishing gears.*

Fishing gear

Fishing gears refers to all types of implements and devices which are used in catching the fish.

Gears can be classified on the basis of their form, function and mode of their operation.

(a) Disabling type

- (i) Wounding gear
- (ii) Stupefying gear
- (iii) Hooks and longlines

(b) Traps and barriers

- (i) Barriers
- (ii) Fish trap

(c) Filtering type

- (i) Dip or lift nets
- (ii) Falling nets
- (iii) Bag nets
- (iv) Drag nets
- (v) Sieve nets
- (vi) Surrounding nets

(d) Entangling type

- (i) Gill nets
- (ii) Trammel nets

Wounding gear

This is a disabling type of gear. It includes bow and arrow and blow gun.

Bow and arrow

- Made up of 2-3 wooden strips tied together with coir.
- Arrow has a barbed end and ball of dry clay in the middle of its length. Rear end of it has a thin string to get back arrow.

Hooks (Fig. 3.1)

- Hooks are usually made up of metal.
- The shank may be short or long.
- The pointed barbed end is known as spear.
- Hooks may be straight or barbed.
- Hooks may have different size and shape. The sizes are indicated by numbers, the bigger the number the smaller the hooks. In shape, hooks may be rounded, flattened, angular, timerick, tuna, double, treble and squid. It can be straight, bent, kirby or reversed.
- The hooks may have an eye or a ring or may be flattened.
- Hooks may or may not have barbs.
- Pole and line fishing is done by barbless hooks.

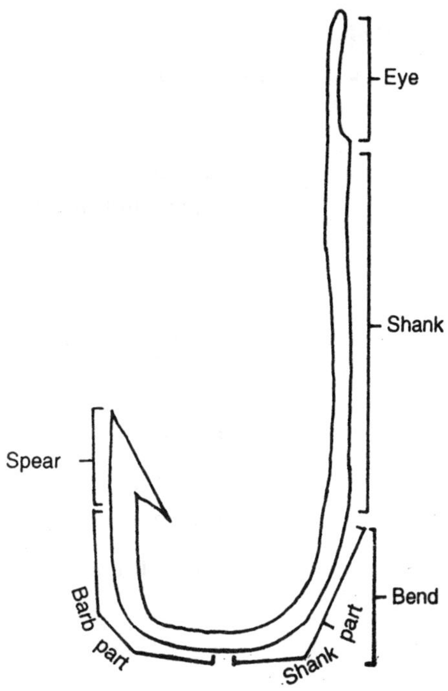

Fig. 3.1. Hook.

Screen barrier (Fig. 3.2)

- In this the bamboo strips are tied together with a coir rope at about 5 mm interval.
- It is placed in the flowing water where it forms a valve and the fishes swimming with water flow are trapped in it.
- It may be round or rectangular.
- It is used to catch the fishes at the outlets or inlets of slow flowing water.

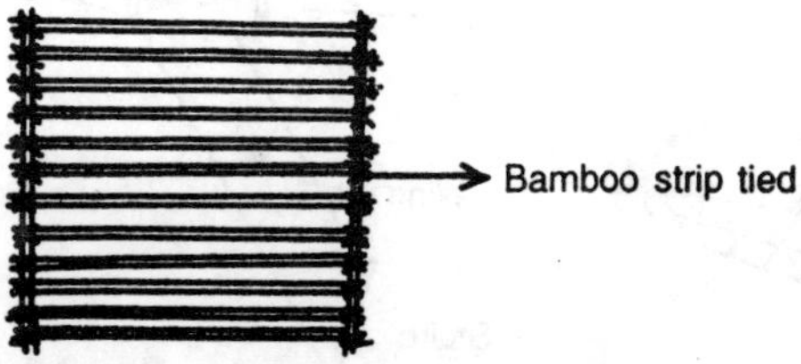

Fig. 3.2. Screen barrier.

Basket trap (Fig. 3.3)

- Made up of flexible bamboo strips.
- Two dome shaped hemispherical baskets are tied together leaving an opening at both ends, which are guarded by flexible bamboo strips.
- Basket along with the bait is placed in the water.
- Fishes entering the basket in search of bait or otherwise are unable to come out.

Cover trap

- It is a conical basket made up of split bamboo pieces with a small circular opening at the top.
- Used in shallow waters to catch the fish from the muddy bottom.
- Height varies from 2-2.5 feet.

Box trap

- Rectangular shaped, made of bamboo strips or netting.
- Opening is present infront. A small opening is also present at the top.
- Front door has a valve like shutter which prevent the escape of trapped animals like crabs and fishes.

Fyke net (Fig.3.4)

- It is a long conical net with elongated caudal end (size varies from 6.0-15.0 m)
- Mouth has a rectangular opening having two vertical sticks on the sides.
- The net has one to several loops and a funnel which prevent the fish from escaping.
- Fishes swimming with the water current are deflected by the wings and guided into the net.
- It is used for spawn and fry collection.

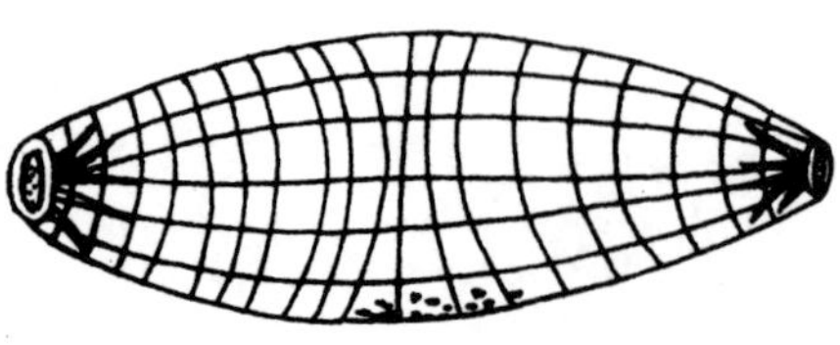

Fig. 3.3. Basket trap.

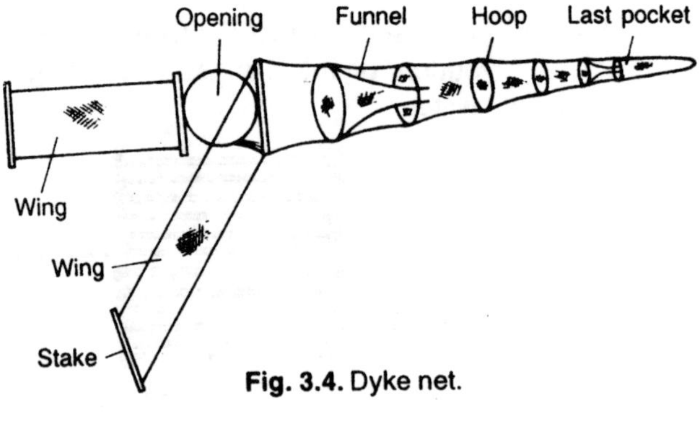

Fig. 3.4. Dyke net.

Dip or lift net (Fig. 3.5)

- These are generally operated with the help of a boat.
- They are dipped in the shore of the stream and then scooped out to capture the fish.
- They are of many types.

Chinese shrimp collection net (Fig. 3.6)

- It is cone shaped, about 25 feet long, made up of hemp fibre with square mouth and narrow caudal end.
- Mouth is about 3.5 feet.
- Mesh size of the mouth is 9 cm while at the caudal end mesh size is 2.5 cm.
- Net is fixed at 90° to the flow of tide.
- A light source or lantern is generally placed at the top of the net to attract shrimps at night time.

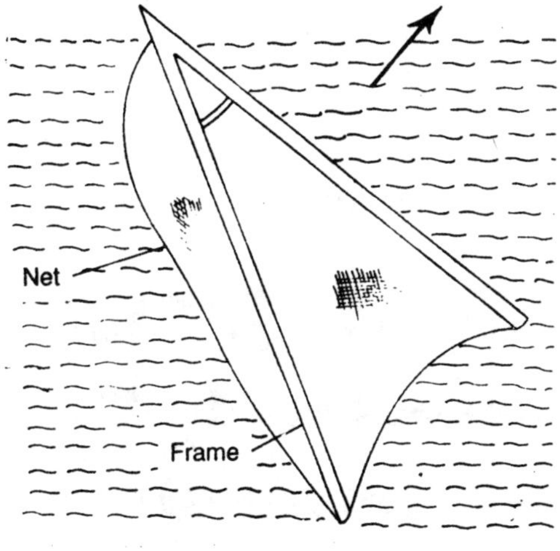

Fig. 3.5. Dip net.

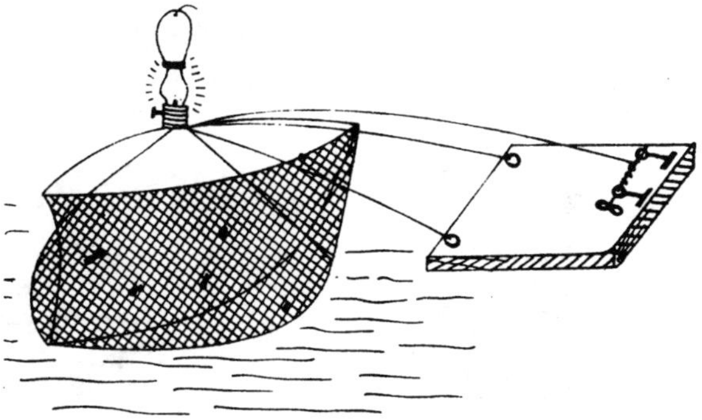

Fig. 3.6. Chinese shrimp collection net.

Stringed cast net (Fig. 3.7)

- It is a simple net of circular shape (large umbrella type), made up of cotton, silken or synthetic fibre.
- Mesh size varies.
- The periphery is provided with sinkers (lead pieces) and apex with a cord.
- It is used for catching fishes from ponds, lakes, rivers and sea coast.
- It is difficult to operate when water is full of weeds or rocks.

Bag net

- It is a triangular tunnel shaped net.
- It is made up of cotton or of synthetic fibre.
- Mouth is kept open with bamboo sticks.
- It is fixed in the water body for catching the fish and fish swimming with the water current enters in the bag.
- They are used normally in running waters and also at night.

Drag net

- These nets are either dragged along the bottom or towed through the water at the desired depth with the help of a boat in big reservoirs, lakes and coastal areas.
- They can also be dragged manually in shallow ponds and back waters.
- They are usually made up of twine synthetic thread or of wire.
- The upper margin is provided with a strong rope and floats and the lower margin is provided with heavy lead sinkers.

Purse seine (Fig. 3.8)

- It is a encircling type of gear.
- Its size ranges from 350-500m, made of synthetic material, rope, wire etc.

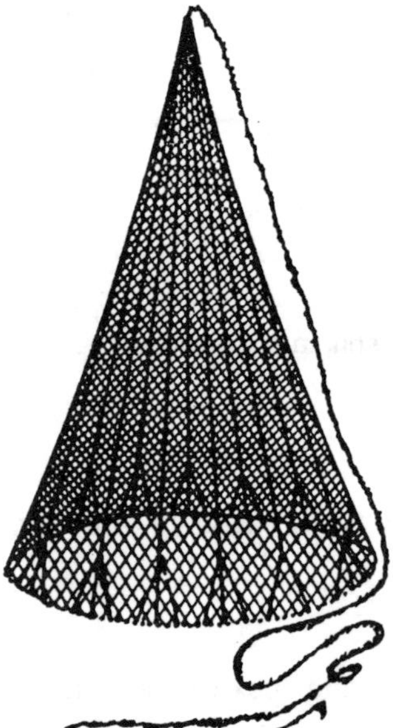

Fig. 3.7. Cast net.

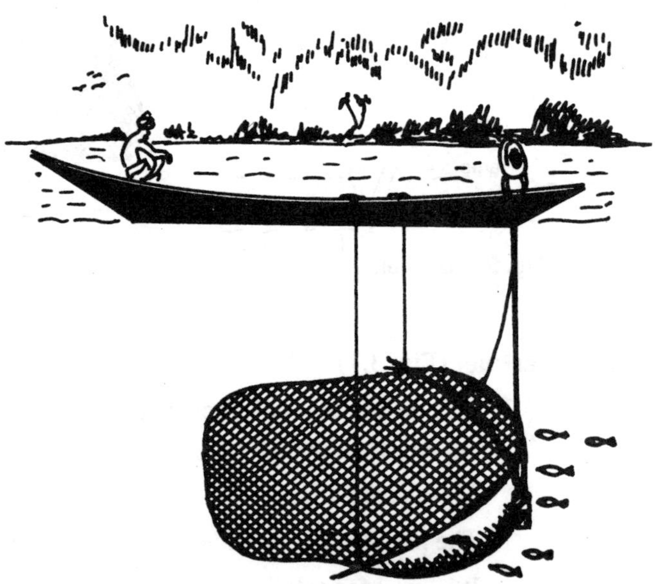

Fig. 3.8. Purse net.

- The upper margin (head line) is provided with foam or plastic floats. Mesh size is generally uniform, larger at head line and smaller at foot line. Another line known as purse line is also present, when this line is pulled, the net assumes the form of a purse like structure.
- It is generally operated from mechanized boats of a power vessel for catching big shoal of fishes.

Gill net (Fig. 3.9)

- Made of cotton or synthetic fibres.
- For catching fish they are fixed in big reservoirs.
- Mesh size varies depending upon the species to be caught.
- Fishes which generally move from one place to another in the water body when try to pass through the net their opercular regions get entangled.

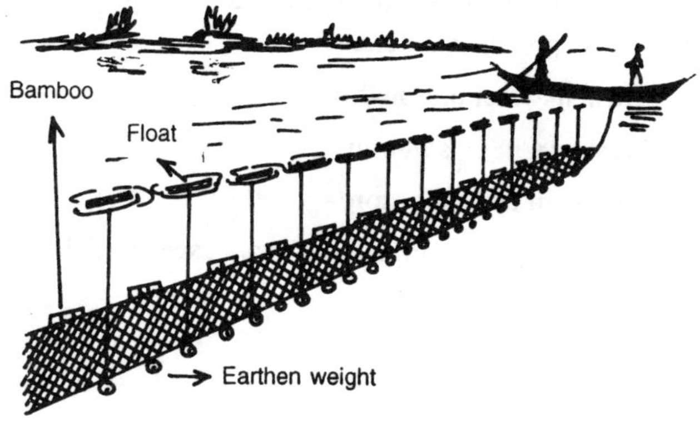

Fig. 3.9. Gill net.

Traditional fishing crafts

1. Dug out canoe (Fig. 3.10)

Made from large logs of wood by scooping out inner part, mainly used in Kerala and Kanara coast. They are 10 to 12m long.

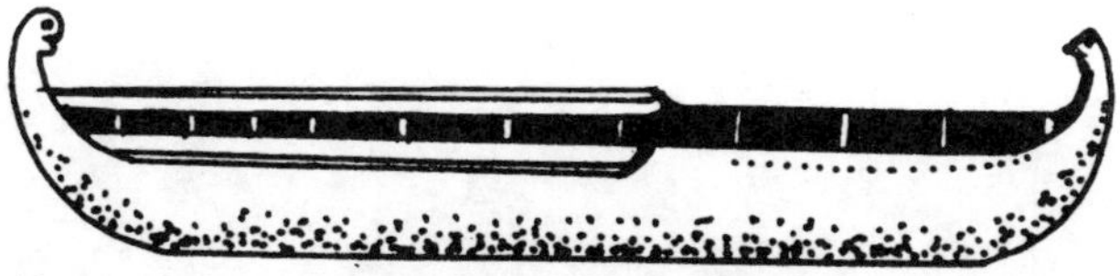

Fig. 3.10. Dug-out canoe.

2. Out trigger canoe (Fig. 3.11)

Canoe with single out trigger used in Kanara in Konkan coast called as Rampani boats used for mackeral fishing operations with rampani net. Size - 15m×3m.

Fig. 3.11. Out-trigger canoe.

Exercise 1 : You are being provided a freshly used cotton/hemp/synthetic net. How you will proceed for its proper maintenance ?

- Wash in water thoroughly
- Wash in $CuSO_4$ solution
- Dry in air and then store

Exercise 2 : Draw diagrams of important crafts and gears used for fishing in your area.

CHAPTER 4

Fish Nutrition

Experiment 4.1 : *To determine and analyse the stomach contents of a given fish*

Materials

(i) Dissecting instruments and dissecting tray.

(ii) Measuring cylinder/centrifuge tubes.

(iii) Microscope

Theory

Analysis of stomach contents of a fish indicate the extent of competition among different fishes and their food preferences.

Procedure

- Obtain a freshly caught fish from its habitat and dissect it immediately for the examination of stomach contents.
- Place the digestive tracts individually in a petridish.
- Separate the stomach and cut open it, flush out the stomach contents with the help of a syringe or wash bottle. Particles still sticking to the stomach walls be removed carefully with a pair of forceps or brush. Use as little water as possible.
- Examine the contents under a dissecting microscope. Separate, identify and count the type and number of organisms present in the stomach contents.
- Remove moisture from the groups of organisms by placing them on a piece of blotting paper for one minute.
- Place the various individuals or groups of individuals in a centrifuge tube containing 5 ml of water, record volume displacement for each.
- Calculate the percentage of total volume of each group of organisms present.
- Fish found in stomach contents should be identified if possible.

Observation

Record the gut content analysis data in the following tabulated form :

Table 10 : Gut Contents Record

Name of the fish species :

Date and time of collection :

Organism/groups of organisms	No. of species	No. of individuals	Volume in ml	% total volume

Experiment 4.2 **:** *To determine the forage ratio for a given fish.*

Theory

It is a ratio of the per cent organisms present in the gut contents of a given fish to the percentage of the same kind of organisms present in the water column/sediment sample depending upon the feeding habit of the fish.

Procedure

- Collect water samples and bottom biota with a suitable sampler.
- Analyse the biota qualitatively and quantitatively (as described in analysis of plankton/benthos).
- Find out the percentage of constituent organisms in each sample.
- Pool the analysed gut data and calculate the ratio and determine the per cent of constituent organisms as follows :

Calculation

$$\text{Forage ratio} = \frac{\text{\% of organisms in the gut contents}}{\text{\% of organisms present in the water/bottom sample}}$$

- If forage ratio is 1, it indicates random selection of food from the environment.
- If forage ratio <1, it indicates avoidance of particular food item.
- If forage ratio > 1, it indicates that the item is actively preferred or chosen by the fish.

Table 11 : Observation table for recording stomach analysis data

Name of the fish :

Date and time of collection :

S.No.	Name and type of food items present in stomach contents	% of each	Organism of each type present in water/ sediment sample	% of each

Experiment 4.3 : *To calculate the amount of feed ingredients required to prepare 100kg of fish feed having 30% protein contents. Utilizing given ingredients.*

Feed ingredients

- Fish meal - protein 41%
- Wheat flour - protein 13.6%

Calculation

<u>Square formula</u>

Wheat flour 13.6% — 11 kg of wheat flour

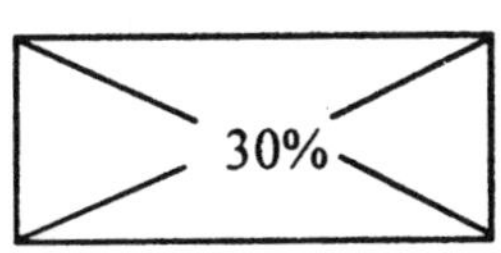

Fish meal 41% — 16.4 kg of fish meal

- Total feed in kg = 11kg (Wheat flour) + 16.4 kg (fish meal) of 30% protein
- Total feed in kg of 30% protein = 27.4
- Wheat flour required for 100 kg fish feed $= \frac{11}{27.4} \times 100$

  $= 40.14$ kg

  $= 40.00$ kg
- Fish meal required for 100kg fish feed $= \frac{16.4}{27.4} \times 100$

  $= 59.85 \quad = 60$ kg

Therefore, take 40 kg of wheat flour and mix with 60 kg of fish meal.

Note : If the number of ingredients is more than two, determine the approximate composition of each ingredient for the preparation of diets for known protein, fat and energy contents etc.— Calculate by linear method on computer.

***Experiment 4.4* :** *Perform an experiment of a given feed to study the growth performance of fish fry/fingerlings.*

Materials

(i) Feed, glass aquaria, balance, hand nets

Procedure

- Stack the aquaria at a fixed place in the room where there is no disturbance.
- Fill the aquaria with dechlorinated tap water (say 10 to 20 L).
- Obtain the fish fry/fingerlings of equal size and divide them into groups of 5 to 10 each.
- Record the weight of the fish fingerlings on a balance and introduce these fingerlings in the aquaria.
- Take the weighed amount of feed to be tested : Make a paste in the petri plate and place it in the aquaria for feeding.
- You can select any rate of feeding (say from 2 to 4% of body weight d^{-1}).
- Continue the experiment with one daily feeding for about 30 days.
- Collect the left over feed and faeces from each aquariam with the help of a siphon. Dry it on blotting paper and record the weight.
- Record the data in the following table.

Table 12 : Observation table for recording feed consumption

Date of experiment :

Name of the student :

Fish species :

Fry/fingerlings/adult fish :

Name of feed :

Feeding level ....% BW d^{-1} of fish

S.No.	Date of feeding	Initial wt. of fish (g)	Wt. of feed given daily (g)	Wt. of left over feed (g)	Wt. of feaces collected (g)

Note : *(i)* *Record the weight of experimental fish at weekly intervals and adjust the feeding rate accordingly.*

(ii) *Collect faecal sample and left over feed separately and daily, keep the sample on a piece of tin foil and dry it in an oven for overnight at 60°C.*

(iii) *For processing the data, for calculations follow the table no. 13.*

Experiment 4.5 **:** *Determination of digestibility of a given diet.*

In fish, direct determination of digestibility is impractical due to the need for quantitative faecal sample collector. So an indirect method using chromic oxide as an inert marker is employed, which is excreted without digestion or loss.

Principle

Feed chromic oxide incorporated diet. Collect faecal samples after a minimum period of feeding (Normally 14 days), Assay the faecal samples and diet for Cr_2O_3 and the percentage dry matter digestibility is calculated from the equation :

$$\text{\% dry matter digestibility} = 100 \times \frac{(1\text{-C})}{B} \times \frac{(1\text{-B})}{(1\text{-C})}$$

Where,

C = g indicator/g dry matter diet

B = g indicator/g dry matter faeces

Preparation of Chromic oxide diet

Take the experimental diet. Add Cr_2O_3 @ 1% and mix with the addition of water until a doughy consistency is reached. The mixture is then made into pellets. The pellets are thoroughly dried in a drying oven overnight with gentle heating. A sample of diet is retained for the analysis of Cr_2O_3 content.

Faecal Sampling

Faecal sample collection

After anaesthesia, apply gentle pressure along the sides of the vent to expel a faecal sample onto a piece of labelled silver foil, avoiding contamination of slime or milt. Only the initial portion expelled part is to be used for digestibility determination. Faecal samples are dried overnight at 80°C, powdered and stored in small plastic tubes.

Measurement

Dried faeces and food samples are powdered. Weigh 50 or 100 mg of each sample accurately and transfer the samples to a dry 100 ml Kjeldahl flask. Add 5 ml concentrated nitric acid (Analar) to each. Flasks are gently shaken to wash down any particles adhering to the sides. Wait for five minutes and then heat the flasks, with occasional shaking to prevent the particles adhering to the sides, until a white precipitate appears (approximately 20 minutes).

Table 13 : Observations for growth parameters

S.No.	Initial wt. of fish (g)	Final wt. of fish(g)	Weekly wt. gain (g)	Weekly dry weight of feaces (g)	Total protein consumed (g)	FCR	SGR	Digestibility (%)	Food consumption/ day in % B.W.	Growth per cent gain in B.W.	Growth per day in %age B.W.	PER

Note : *(i) Calculate the total amount of protein consumed in (g) from the proximate composition of feed*

(ii) Calculate FCR, SGR, Digestibility (%), food consumption per day in percentage body weight, growth per day in percentage body weight, growth per cent gain in body weight (See exercise 1 for calculations)

Remove the flasks from the heater and cool them. Add 3 ml of perchloric acid to each flask and then reheat the flasks until the greenish white colour changes to a red-orange colour (usually 30-40 minutes). To ensure the reaction is complete, heat the samples for another 10 minutes, cool the flasks slightly and add 50 ml of distilled water to terminate the reaction. Cool the flasks to room temperature and transfer the contents of each flask to a clean 100 ml volumetric flask and make up the volume to 100 ml with distilled water.

Wait for 10 minutes to allow the formation of precipitates of organic matter present, if any. Take a suitable aliquot from each flask into a plastic cuvette. Read optical density at 350 nm on a spectrophotometer. Use distilled water as blank (for zeroing).

Calculations

The standard curve for the wet digestion method may be expressed by the equation :

$$Y = 0.2089\,X + 0.0032 \qquad \text{Eq. (1)}$$

Where,

Y = Optical density at 350 nm

X = Chromic oxide content of the sample (mg/100 ml)

The values obtained for faecal samples and a sample of diet used may then be substituted in equation (1) to calculate the % dry matter digestibility.

Proximate Analysis of feed/fish/tissues/faeces

Proximate analysis is the determination of categories of compounds present in a mixture i.e. the composition of protein, carbohydrate and fat (AOAC, 1995).

Experiment 4.6 : *Determination of % moisture and dry matter.*

Principle

Loss in weight on drying is determined to calculate % moisture and dry matter.

Materials

(i) Oven maintained at 103°C±2°C

Procedure

- Take a glass container dry it in an oven at 103±2°C for 30 minutes.
- After drying, place the container in a desiccator for 45-60 minutes.
- When cool, record the weight of the container.
- Add about 5g of the sample in the container and weigh accurately.
- Place the container in an oven maintained at 103±2°C for 6 hrs.
- Cool the container in a desiccator for 45-60 minutes.
- Weigh the container again

Calculations

$$\% \text{ moisture} = \frac{\text{Wet weight of the sample - dry weight of the sample}}{\text{Wet weight of the sample}} \times 100$$

Dry matter = 100 – % moisture

Experiment 4.7 : *Determination of crude protein by Kjeldahl method*

Principle

Digestion of organic matter of a test portion by sulphuric acid in the presence of a catalyst. The nitrogen of the test portion is converted into ammonium salts. The reaction mixture is made alkaline; distilled and the collected ammonia is titrated against acid. The nitrogen contents are calculated by multiplying with an international protein factor (6.25), the crude protein content is obtained.

Materials

(i) Conc. H_2SO_4

(ii) Potassium sulphate solid (K_2SO_4)

(iii) Cupric sulphate solid ($CuSO_4 . 5H_2O$)

(iv) H_2SO_4 titrant 0.01N

(Dissolve 0.274 ml of conc. H_2SO_4 to 1 L. Take 100 ml of it and dilute to 1.0 L)

(v) Methyl red indicator

(Dissolve 0.1 g of the indicator in 60 ml of alcohol and make the volume to 100 ml).

(vi) NaOH 0.01 N

(Dissolve 4 g of NaOH in distilled water and make the volume to 1L. Cool and dilute 100 ml of it to 1 L).

(vii) Micro Kjeldahl assembly.

Procedure

- Take 0.1-2.0 g of accurately weighed sample in a 500 ml Kjeldahl digestion flask.
- Add to it 0.5-5.0 g of digestion mixture (K_2SO_4 and $CuSO_4$ in the ratio of 9:1) and 10-30 ml conc. H_2SO_4.
- Digest the sample by heating the flask till the sample turns light green and only 2-2.5 ml of the sample is left in the flask.
- Cool and make the volume to 100 ml by adding distilled water.
- Take 10 ml of this solution in a distillation flask, add to it 15-20 ml of NaOH solution (40% w/v).

- Distill and collect the ammonia liberated in 10 ml of 0.01 N H_2SO_4 with 2-3 drops of methyl red indicator.
- Collect approximately 40 ml of the distillate and titrate again with 0.01N NaOH till end point (blue colour) appears.

Calculations

$$\% \text{ crude protein} = \frac{V \times 0.00014 \times D \times 100 \times 6.25}{w \times A}$$

Where,

V = volume of 0.01 N H_2SO_4 taken - volume of 0.01 N NaOH used

D = dilution factor = Volume made in volumetric flask after digestion

W = weight (g) of sample

A = aliquot taken

Experiment 4.8 **:** *Determination of crude fat.*

Principle

Sample is extracted with diethyl ether in a continuous extractor. The solvent is distilled off. The residue is dried and weighed.

Materials

(i) Anhydrous diethyl ether/Petroleum benzene

(ii) Soxhlet's apparatus

(iii) Water bath

Procedure

- Take 3 g of dried and powdered sample in a filter paper pouch (Whatman No. 40).
- Prepare a pouch of the Whatman filter paper permitting rapid passage of ether. Weigh the pouch.
- Extract the sample for fat with ether/petroleum benzene at 60-80°C in Soxhlet's apparatus.
- Continue the extraction for 6-8 hours at a condensation rate of 2-3 drops/sec.
- After extraction, dry the sample for 30 minutes at 100°C.
- Cool and record the final weight of the pouch.

Calculations

Fat contents mg/100g of dried sample = Wi-Wf

Where, Wi = initial wt of the sample

Wf = final wt of the sample

$$\% \text{ fat} = \frac{\text{Wt. of fat (g)}}{\text{Wt. of sample (g)}} \times 100$$

Experiment 4.9 : *Determination of nitrogen free extract (NFE)*

Percent NFE is calculated by subtracting the sum of % protein, fat and moisture from 100.

% NFE = 100 - (crude protein + fat + moisture)

Experiment 4.10 : *Determination of Ash contents*

Materials

(i) Muffle furnace

(ii) Silicon crucibles, A pair of tongs

Procedure

- Take 5.0g of the dried and powdered sample in a silicon crucible-Record the total weight.
- Incinerate it in a furnace preheated to 550°C for 4 h.
- Transfer the curcible with a pair of tongs to the desiccator.
- Cool it and then weigh it again.

Calculations

$$\% \text{ ash} = \frac{\text{Ash weight}}{\text{Sample wt.}} \times 100$$

Note : *Before using the crucible, place it in the furnace at 550°C for 1 h. Remove it and keep it in a desiccator for one hour and record its weight.*

Experiment 4.11 : *Determination of crude fibre*

Principle

Determination of crude fibre is based on treating the moisture and fat free samples successively with dilute acid and alkali

Materials required

1. Tall spoutless beakers (1 L capacity)
2. Bulb condensers
3. Hot plate
4. Muslin cloth
5. Hot air oven

6. Muffle furnace
7. Silica crucibles
8. Vacuum pump
9. Sulphuric acid 1.25% (v/v)
10. Sodium hydroxide 1.25% (w/v)

* Crude fibre estimation apparatus consisting of hot plates, six spoutless beakers and six bulb type of condensors is also available with many firms (Fig. 4.1)

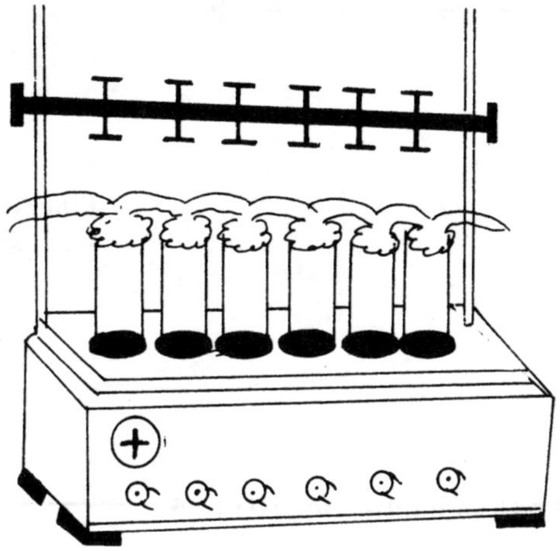

Fig. 4.1. Crude fibre estimator.

Procedure (See also flow diagram)

- Take 1.0-2.0 g of moisture and fat free sample in the spoutless beaker and add to it 200 ml of 1.25% H_2SO_4.
- Place the beaker on hot plate and allow to reflux for 30 minutes. Shake the contents after every five minutes.
- After 30 minutes remove the beaker from the hot plate and filter the contents using a piece of muslin cloth. Use vacuum or suction pumps, if required.
- Wash the residue with hot water (4-5 times).
- Transfer the residue to the same beaker and add 200 ml of 1.25% NaOH solution, reflux again for 30 minutes.
- After 30 minutes filter again through the muslin cloth and wash the residue first with 0.5% HCl and then with hot water.
- Transfer the residue in preweighed crucible and dry to a constant weight in hot air oven (100°C).

- Weigh the contents (x) and ignite at 550°C for 4h.
- Cool and weigh again (y).

Calculate % crude fibre as follows :

$$\% \text{ Crude fibre} = \frac{(x\text{-}y) \times 100}{\text{Sample weight}}$$

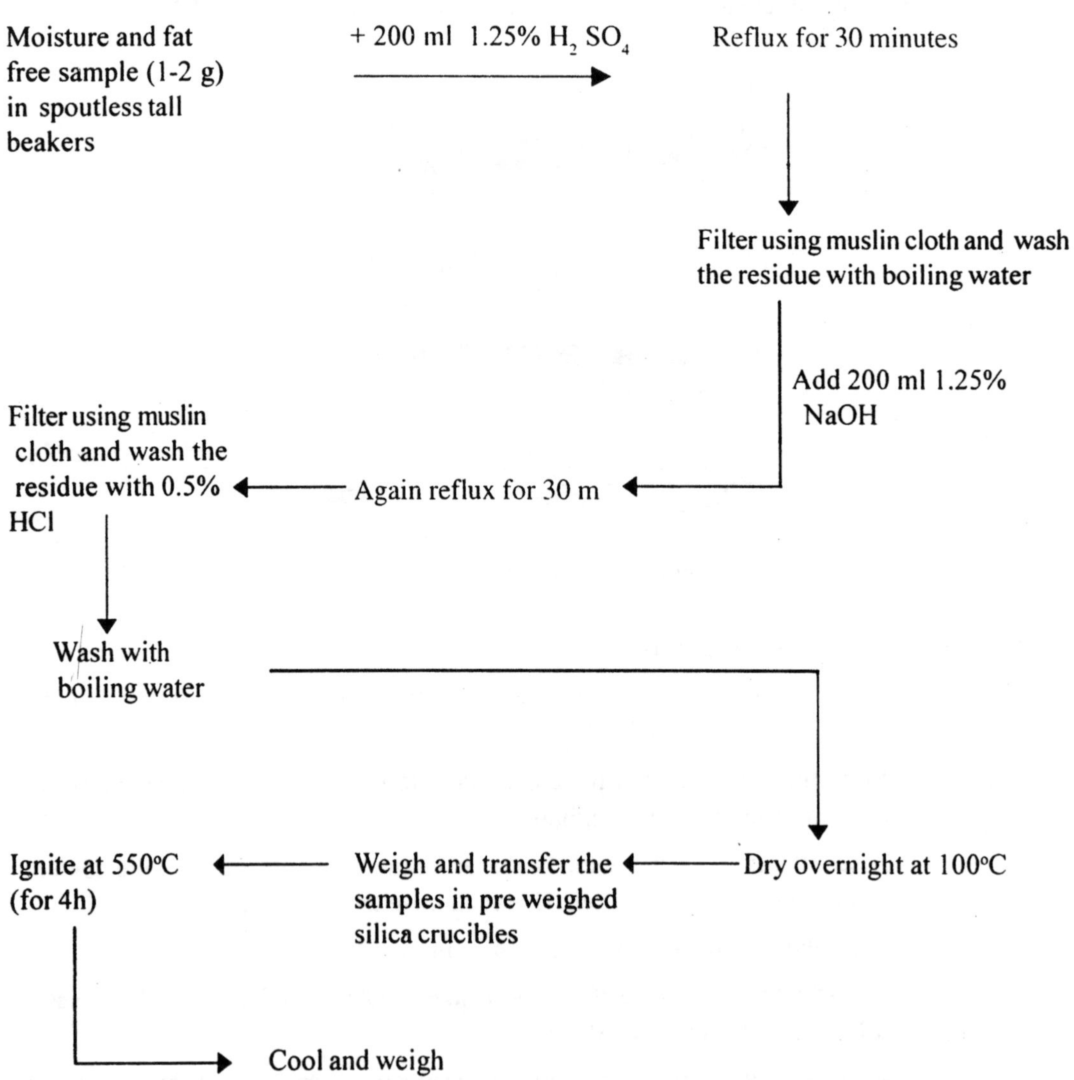

Flow diagram showing the procedure for the estimation/determination of crude fibre contents

Experiment 4.12 : *Determination of energy (E) contents of fish/feed*

Calculate the energy contents from the chemical composition of the given material as follows:

The caloric values in terms of K cal g^{-1} are calculated using the average caloric conversion factors of 9.45, 4.10 and 5.65 K cal g^{-1} for fat, carbohydrate and protein respectively (Henken *et al.* 1986).

OR

$$E\ (K\ J g^{-1}) = 0.2364 \times \text{protein}\ (\%) + 0.3954 \times \text{fat}\ (\%) + 0.1715 \times \text{carbohydrates}\ (\%)$$

Gross energy can also be determined directly using a Bomb calorimeter.

Exercise 1: Calculate the following parameters from the given data :

(i) Growth (per cent gain in body weight)

(ii) Growth per day in percentage body weight

(iii) Digestibility or food absorption efficiency (%)

(iv) Food consumption per day in percentage body weight

(v) Feed conversion ratio (FCR)

(vi) Gross conversion efficiency (GCE)

(vii) Protein efficiency ratio (PER)

Wo or W_1 = Live weight of the fish at the beginning of the experiment = 4.6g

Wt or W_2 = Live weight of the fish at the end of the experiment = 4.9g

t = duration of the experiment = 7 days

Dry weight of total food given = 0.60 (g)

C = Total quantity of food consumed = 0.60 (g)

Weight gain at the end of the experiment = 0.3 g

Total protein fed = 0.075 (g)

Calculations

Growth (per cent gain in body weight)

$$= \frac{\text{Final wt. - Initial wt.}}{\text{Initial wt.}} \times 100 = \frac{4.9 - 4.6}{4.6} \times 100 = 6.52$$

Growth per day in percentage body weight

$$= \frac{2(Wt\text{-}Wo)}{t\,(w_t + w_o)} \times 100 = \frac{2(0.3) \times 100}{7(9.5)} = 0.90$$

Digestibility or food absorption efficiency FAE %

$$= \frac{\text{Dry weight of food - dry weight of faeces}}{\text{Dry weight of food}}$$

$$\text{FAE(\%)} = \frac{(0.60 - 0.30)}{0.60} \times 100 = 50\%$$

Food consumption per day in percentage body weight

$$\text{Formula} = \frac{2C}{t\,(W_t + W_o)} \times 100 = \frac{2\times0.6\times100}{7(9.5)} = \frac{1.2\times100}{66.5} = 1.80$$

Feed conversion ratio (FCR)

$$\text{FCR (g)} = \frac{\text{Weight of food given}}{\text{Weight gain of fish}}$$

$$\text{FCR (g)} = \frac{0.60}{0.30} = 2.0$$

Gross conversion effeciency

$$\text{GCE} = \frac{\text{Weight gain (Live)}}{\text{Weight of food consumed}}$$

$$\text{GCE} = \frac{0.30}{0.60} = 0.50$$

Protein efficiency ratio (PER)

$$\text{PER} = \frac{\text{Gain in body weight live}}{\text{Total protein intake}}$$

$$\text{PER} = \frac{0.3}{0.075} = 4.0$$

Specific growth rate

i) $$\frac{\text{Log } W_t - \log W_0}{D} \times 100$$

$$\frac{\log 4.9 - \log 4.6}{7} \times 100$$

ii) or $\dfrac{\ln W_t - \ln W_0}{D} \times 100$

$$\frac{\ln 4.9 - \ln 4.6}{7} \times 100$$

Exercise 2 : Calculate the following parameters :

(a) growth (b) growth rate (c) arithmetic mean body weight

(d) specific growth rate

Where,

$W_o = 10g$, $W_t = 185g$, $t = 80$ days

Ans.

(a) Growth = dw = Wt - Wo

dw = 185-10 = 175g

(b) Growth rate $= \dfrac{dw}{dt} = \dfrac{Wt - Wo}{t} = \dfrac{175}{80}$

$= 2.1875 \text{ g d}^{-1}$

(c) Arithmetic mean body weight = BWa

$$= \frac{W_t + W_o}{2}$$

$$= \frac{185 + 10}{2} = 97.5$$

(d) Specific growth rate (SGR)

$$= \frac{\ln W_t - \ln W_o}{t} \times 100$$

$$= \frac{5.220 - 2.30}{80} \times 100 = 3.646 \text{ \% BW d}^{-1}$$

CHAPTER 5

Management of Fish Health and Hygiene

Poor growth and mortality of fishes due to diseases is commonly encountered in fish ponds. Like the other animals, fishes are also prone to the attack of various disease causing organisms. This is one of the most acute problem faced by the fish culturists.

Majority of the diseases of fishes are caused by bacteria, viruses and protozoa. Besides this, fishes are also attacked by fungi, worms, parasitic copepods and other blood sucking external parasites such as, leeches and arthropods etc. It should be borne in mind that only such diseases can be controlled where the symptoms are recognizable. Contamination of environment where the fish lives and also due to imbalanced diet or wrong formulations also results in poor health of fishes (See plates 9, 10 and 11).

Experiment 5.1 **:** *To identify the important fish diseases and disorders.*

(a) BACTERIAL DISEASES

(i) **Name of the disease** : Fin-rot or tail-rot

Causative agent : Bacteria e.g. *Aeromonas* and *Pseudomonas*

It is common in ponds which are rich in bottom muck and receive domestic sewage and cattle washings etc.

Symptoms

White line appears on the margins of fins which gradually extends to the base, fin rays become brittle, breaks on handling and fins ultimately gets destroyed.

Treatment

(i) Dip the fish for one minute in a copper sulphate solution of 500 ppm (5mg of $CuSO_4$ in one litre of water).

(ii) In a very severe infection, remove the fins with the help of surgical equipment then treat the wound with one per cent solution of silver nitrate and then keep the fish in a solution of potassium dichromate (1:25000) for recovery of wound (7 days).

PLATE 9

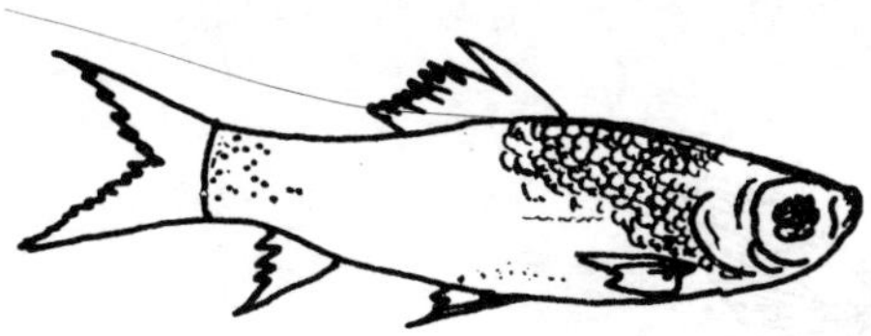

Tail and fin rot disease

Dropsy

Furunculosis in trout

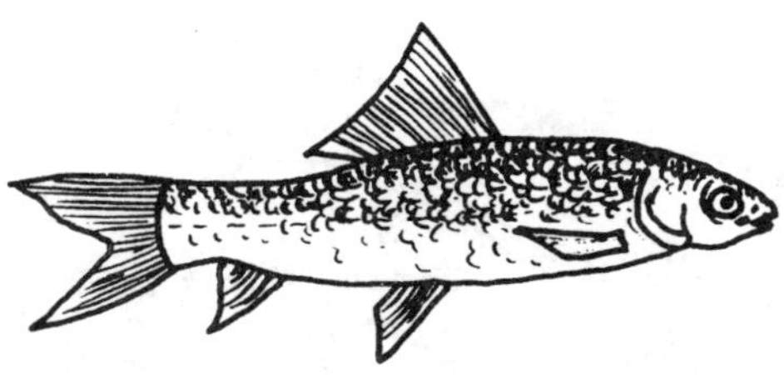

Myxosporidiosis

Cyclochaetosis

Ichthyophthiriasis (carp attacked by white spot)

PLATE 10

Pox disease in carp

Boil disease in *Barbus barbus*

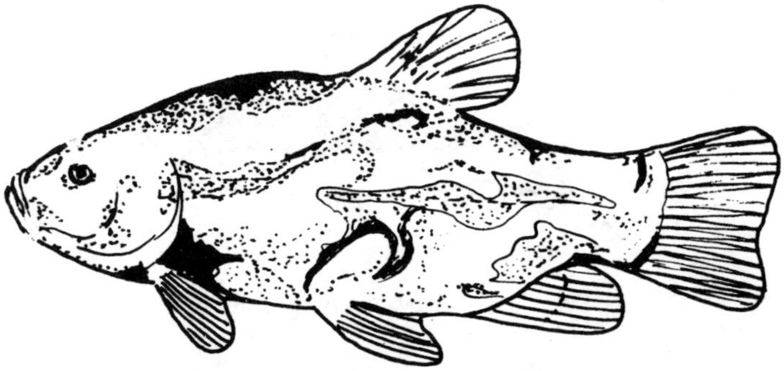

Costiasis in *Tinca tinca*

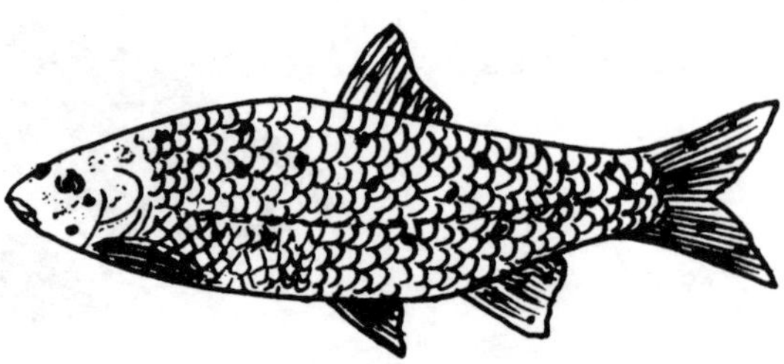

Black spot disease

PLATE 11

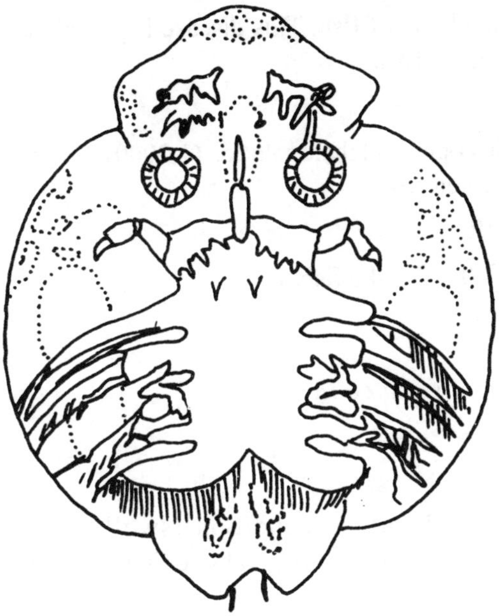

Argulus

Gyrodactylus

Dactylogyrus

Fish leech—*Piscicola*

Fish leech—*Hemiclepsis*

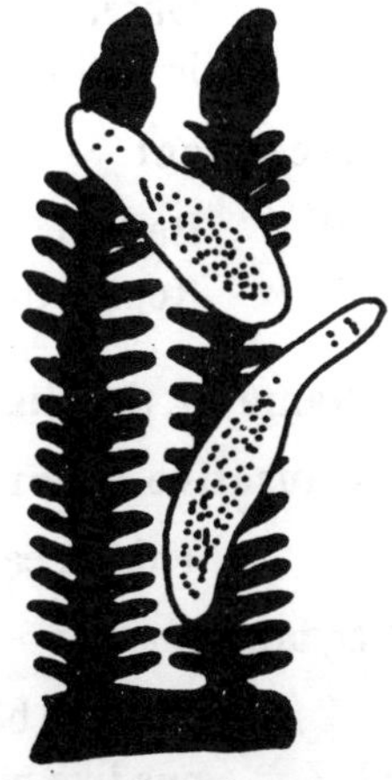

Dactylogyrus at the gill sheet

(ii) **Name of the disease** : Ulcer disease

Symptoms

Observe open sores or ulcers on the body of fish. This disease is prevalent in Indian major carps and other culturable fishes.

Treatment

(i) Give dip treatment for one minute in copper sulphate solution (1:2000). Continue the treatment for 3-4 days for complete cure.

OR

(ii) Mix oxytetracycline in fish food @ 0.075 g /kg fish/day.

(iii) **Name of the disease** : Dropsy

Causative agent : *Pseudomonas punctata*

Cause heavy mortality of carps.

Symptoms

Observe-scale protrusion and exophthalmic condition (swollen eyes), accumulation of yellow or pink fluid in the body cavity and swelling of the belly.

Treatment

(i) Give a dip treatment for two minutes in a 5 ppm solution of potassium permanganate.

(iv) **Name of the disease** : Eye disease

Causative agent : *Aeromonas liquefaciens*

It generally attacks medium and large-sized catla on optic nerves and brain.

Symptoms

Observe eyes with vascularised cornea, which becomes opaque during severe infection, eye balls get decayed.

Treatment

(i) Bath the fish for 2 h in an antibiotic solution of chloromycetin (8-10 mg l^{-1}). Repeat the treatment for 2-3 days.

(v) **Name of the disease** : Furunculosis

Causative agent : *Aeromonas salmonicida*

This disease occurs in culturable salmons and trouts.

Symptoms

Observe boils on the sides of fish, when these boils burst they release blood and pus like material. Observe the haemorrhage at the base of the fins, darkening of skin. Fishes suffering from this disease can be seen gathering at pond outlet.

Treatment

(i) Prevent the contamination of water supply by wild fish and maintain strict hygienic condition. Ponds should be disinfected with quicklime or calcium cyanide. Remove dead fish stock showing furunculosis and destroy them at a distant place.

(ii) On first day feed sulphadiazine @ 0.22g (active)/kg/day followed by 0.11 g (active)/kg/day for next nine days.

(b) VIRAL DISEASES

(vi) **Name of the disease** : DNA virus disease

Causative organism : Channel catfish virus (CCV) occurs in culturable catfishes

Symptoms

Observe loss of equilibrium, hanging vertically and show spiral swimming activity. Haemorrhage of visceral organs may also be seen.

Treatment

No effective treatment is available.

(vii) **Name of the disease** : Spring Viraemia of carp (SVC)

Causative organism : *Rhabdovirus carpio*

Symptoms

Observe dark colour of the body of the host. Distended abdomen. Haemorrhage of gills and skin. Loss of balance can also be observed.

Treatment

No effective treatment is available.

(c) FUNGAL DISEASES

(viii) **Name of the disease** : Water mold disease or saprolegniasis

Causative organism : *Saprolegnia parasitica*

It is a very common disease occurring in most of the cultured fishes.

Symptoms

Observe tuft of woolly grey white hair (cotton-wool) like outgrowth in the affected region (fins, eyes, gills and also mouth), ulceration or exfoliation on the skin of fish, haemorrhage and blindness.

Treatment

A variety of disinfectants such as copper sulphate, malachite green, potassium permanganate, formalin or common salt may be used.

(i) Pick out the infected fish and treat the affected portion by touching disinfectant solution like iodine/potassium dichromate (1:10/1% solution). Afterwards give a dip treatment in a solution of potassium dichromate (1:25,000), and keep the fish in it for 7 days

OR

Give a dip treatment for 3 seconds in a solution of malachite green (1:10000)

OR

Give a dip treatment for 5-10 minutes in a common salt solution (3%) or give a dip treatment in copper sulphate solution (5: 10000).

OR

Give a dip treatment in a solution of potassium permanganate (1:1000) for 60-90 minutes.

(ix) **Name of the disease** : Gill-rot or *Branchiomycosis*

Causative organism : *Branchiomyces sanguinis*

This disease usually occurs during the summer season and very common in densely stocked ponds, where there is abundance of phytoplankton and organic matter.

Symptoms

Observe pale gills and red coloured patches on the gills.

Treatment

Avoid dense stocking and pollution of water. Reduce supplementary feeding during summer. Add more water in the ponds. Add 50 to 100 kg/ha of quick lime. Give a dip treatment to infected fish in 3-5% solution of common salt.

OR

Use 5 ppm $KMnO_4$ solution for 5-10 minutes.

OR

Give a bath treatment in copper sulphate (1:10000) solution for 10-30 minutes.

OR

Bath the fish in Benzalkonium chloride (1-4 ppm) for 1h.

(d) PROTOZOAN DISEASES

(x) **Name of the disease** : White spot disease OR 'Ich' OR *Ichthyophthiriasis*

Causative organism : *Ichthyophthirius multifilis* (ciliated protozoan)

This disease is very common in fresh water fishes such as carps, trout and other young fishes.

Symptoms

Observe the presence of small (0.1-1 mm) whitish cysts (spots) on the skin, gills and fins. This disease can also be identified if fishes are seen rubbing their body against some objects in ponds. As the parasites are under the epidermis, therefore, it is not easy to get rid of the disease.

Treatment

(i) Bathe the fish in methylene blue 2 ppm (for 5 days) or make a formaline solution (1:5000 or 1:4000) and give a dip treatment (for 5-7 days)

OR

(ii) Injection of quinine hydrochloride @ 10-20 ppm (repeated therapy : depending on severity of case)

OR

(iii) Combination of Malachite green (0.5ppm - 1.0 ppm) and formaldehyde (50 ppm) is more effective and may be used as a flush treatment.

OR

(iv) Common salt solution (3:1000)

OR

(v) Pyridyl mercuric acetate (30:1000)

(xi) **Name of the disease** : *Cylochaetosis* and *Trichodiniasis*

Causative agent : *Cylochaeta* and *Trichodina indica*

These protozoan parasites attack the fry of Indian major carps. Parasities multiply very rapidly, therefore, these can be collected in hundreds from the gills and the body of the hosts.

Symptoms

Uneasiness due to irritation in the gills and respiratory trouble, secrete excessive slime on the gills and body. Dark pigmentation on the skin can also be seen and ultimately the fry dies.

Treatment

Dip treatment in a salt solution (1 to 3% depending on the size of fry) cures the fish. Repeat the treatment for 3 to 4 consecutive days.

(xii) **Name of the disease** : *Myxosporidiosis*

Causative organism : *Myxobolus, Myxidium*

Protozoan parasites attack the fry and fingerlings of Indian major carps and common carp belonging to the size ranging from 40 to 150 mm.

Symptoms

Observe minute pin head like white cysts on the fins and body, white patches on the gills are also visible. Infected fry and fingerlings become weak.

Treatment

Remove the severely affected fish and feed the remaining stock well to control the disease.

(xiii) **Name of the disease** : Pox disease

Causative organism : Sporozoans

Symptoms

Observe small milky white spots about 1-2 mm above the skin.

Treatment

Separate the fishes and give intra peritonial injection of Arycil i.e. 1% solution of Arsenic compound.

(xiv) **Name of the disease** : Knot disease

Causative organism : *Myxobolus luciopercae* (sporozoan)

It is mostly seen occurring in common carp species.

Symptoms

Observe small knots on the skin.

Treatment

No effective treatment is available. Infected fish should be eradicated and destroyed.

(xv) **Name of the disease** : *Myxoboliasis tubero-ulcerosis* OR Boil disease OR *Ulceration*

Causative organism : *Myxobolus pfeifferi* (sporozoan)

Symptoms

Observe boils on the body parts of common carp. In other fishes gills and other parts are also affected. Size of the boil may vary from a tiny one to the size of a nut or hen's egg.

Treatment

(i) Prepare a solution of common salt (3%) and bath the infected fish.

OR

(ii) Prepare a solution of formalin (1:2500) and give a dip treatment for 10 minutes.

(xvi) **Name of the disease** : Whirling disease or tumbling disease

Causative organism : *Myxosoma cerebralis*

Symptoms

Observe deformed oral region, bending of caudal region and blackening of tail region in trouts. Note, loss of equilibrium. The young fishes whirl around and fall on the bottom.

Treatment

Eradicate by destroying all the infected fishes with the help of quicklime application @ 2000 kg/ha.

(xvii) **Name of the disease** : Costiasis

Causative organism : *Costia necatrix* (Flagellate)

These parasites live on the skin, fins and also gills.

Symptoms

Observe the bluish/slimy coating on the skin, fins and gills of young carps and salmonid fry. Irregular lesions and red patches on the skin can also be seen.

Treatment

(i) Bath the fish in a 3% solution of common salt.

(ii) Make formalin solution (4 ppm) and give a bath treatment for 10 minutes.

(e) DISEASES CAUSED BY TREMATODES

(xviii) **Name of the disease** : Black spot disease or Diplostamiasis

Causative organism : *Diplostomum* spp.

Symptoms

Observe small black nodules (1-5 mm diameter) on skin, muscles and fins in carps.

Treatment

Give a dip treatment in a solution of picric acid (3:1,00000) for 1 hour and feed Di-n-butyl tin oxide @ 0.25 g/100 kg fish.

(xix) **Name of the disease** : Worm cataract

Causative organism : *Hemistomum spathaceum*

Symptoms

Observe accumulation of watery fluid in the eye and white dots because of the presence of little worms between lens and lens capsule.

Treatment

Give a dip treatment in a solution of potassium antimonyl tartrate (1.5 mg l^{-1}).

(xx) **Name of the diseases** : *Dactylogyrosis* and *Gyrodactylosis*

Causative organisms : *Dactylogyrus* and *Gyrodactylus*

These gill flukes causes great harm in carp nurseries by attacking skin, gills of the fry. They also attack catfishes. Parasites feed on blood, and thin capillaries of the gills.

Symptoms

Observe dropping of fins, fading of colour, peeling of skin, falling of scales, abundant mucus. The affected fish moves near the pond margins and rubs its body against the pond banks and finally the fish dies.

Treatment

Give a bath in a saline solution (2-5% common salt solution) for 3-4 days consecutively (1% for fry). Either drain the pond or heavy liming is done @ 2500 kg ha^{-1}. After liming, leave the pond unused for some months.

(xxi) **Name of the parasite** : *Acanthocephala*

Symptoms

Mainly found in Indian major carps (Catla, Rohu, Mrigal), observe spiny headed worms which remain attached to the walls of the intestine and cause severe wounds.

Treatment

Di-n-butyl tin oxide

(xxii) **Name of the disease** : *Ligulosis*

Causative organism : *Ligula intistinalis*

Symptoms

This disease is caused by yellowish-white tape worms. The worm lives inside the intestine of cyprinids. Therefore, it feeds on the food consumed by the fish, retardation of growth occurs.

(f) DISEASE CAUSED BY WORMS

Symptoms

When fishes appear dull and sickly it is presumed that they are infected by a variety of disease causing agents, such as Acanthocephala, flatworms and nematodes. In cases when the fishes are infected by nematodes and cestodes, alimentary canal of such fishes appear swollen and chocked with worms.

Treatment

Give a dip treatment in Picric acid 3:1,00,000 for 60 minutes, and feed Di-n-butyl tin oxide @ 0.25 g/kg of fish/day is helpful in controlling the infection.

(g) DISEASE CAUSED BY HIRUDINEA

Leeches : These are blood sucking ectoparasities of fishes

Causative organism : *Hemiclepsis* sp.

Symptoms

The fish shows abnormal swimming due to irritation as the parasites feeds on the blood of fish.

Treatment

(i) Give a dip treatment in a solution of glacial acetic acid (1:1000).

Piscicola and *Myzobdella* are common leeches which infect the fishes. They possess well developed large suckers to attach themselves to the body of fishes for sucking blood. They may inhabit fresh or less brackish water. In case of heavy infection they cause haemorrhage and anaemia.

Treatment

(i) Drain and flush the ponds to dryness. Use Dylox @ 0.5-1.0 ppm for 5 days. Remove the parasites manually by forceps or by rubbing cloth. Treat with Dipterex @ 0-30 ppm for 3 days.

(h) DISEASES CAUSED BY THE COPEPODS (CRUSTACEANS)

Causative organism : *Argulus* (carplice)

The parasite attaches itself to the skin of the fish at the base of fins.

Symptoms

Loss of scale, presence of red spots on the skin and damage the gills. The infection of carplice causes heavy mortalities in the nurseries.

Treatment

(i) Give a dip treatment in a solution of formalin (500 ppm) for 30 minutes.

(ii) Remove the parasites by fine forceps and then give a dip treatment in $KMnO_4$ solution. Thereafter, a bath treatment in glacial acetic (1:1000) acid solution for 4-5 minutes, then a bath in common salt (1%) solution for 60 minutes. Ponds may be treated by adding potassium permanganate (0.2-0.3 g/gallon of water).

(iii) 0.015g of lindane per cubic meter of water is also highly effective.

(iv) or Benzene hexachloride (BHC) at 0.5 ppm.

(v) Alternatively erection of bamboo poles at many places in the ponds would assist the fishes to rub their body to remove the parasites.

Name of the parasite : *Lernaea* spp. (Anchor worm)

Symptoms

The anterior region of *Lernaea* i.e. head and mouth totally buried in the infected fish skin. The infected fish show erratic swimming activity of the fish and moribund appearance. It mainly attacks carps and air breathing fishes.

Treatment

Its control is quite difficult because lernea has chitinous exposed part in the water and the anterior head region and respiratory part is embedded inside the host tissue. Therefore, lower concentration of systemic poisons/chemicals can not give full relief to the host.

- Control manually by using fine forceps for removing the parasite.
- Dip treatment in 3-5% of common salt.
- Bath treatment in 250 ppm formaline for 1 h every 3 weeks (15-20 days).
- Gammexane 0.1 to 0.2 ppm treatment.

- Lexone 2.7 ppm weekly (72 to 96 h) at 3 weeks interval.
- Lindane 0.1 ppm for 72 to 96 h
- Chlorine 1 ppm for 3 days.

Name of the parasite : *Argulus* (fish lice)

Symptoms

The parasite penetrate in the skin and release cytotoxin resulting in the ulcer and heamorrhage. The fish lice feeds on blood of the fish. Fish becomes exhausted, loss of equilibrium, zig-zag swimming and flashing movements. It attacks carps and air-breathing fishes.

Control

- Control manually.
- Use always filtered water in culture ponds.
- Clean, flush and completely dry the pond.
- Use Ammonium chloride @ 500 ppm for 24 h
- Balsam of peru @ 40 ppm for 3 h
- Dip treatment in DDT @ 10 ppm for 15-20 seconds.
- Dylox @ 0.25 ppm is greatly effective and biodegradable.
- Dip treatment in lysol @ 2000 ppm upto 15 seconds.
- Malathion @ 0.25/Methyl parathion 0-12 ppm.
- $KMnO_4$ @ 10 ppm for 30 minutes.
- Pyrethrum @ 10 ppm of aqueous extract for 10-15 minutes.

Prevention of ectoparasite is better than using chemicals for cure because higher concentrations result in mass mortality in pond treatments. Some chemicals like malathion and methylparathion are toxic to fish and human life.

(i) MISCELLANEOUS DISEASES AND DISORDERS

Name of the disease : Gas bubble disease

Causative factor :

This disease occurs when nitrogen in a waterbody exceeds 125 per cent, rapid fluctuation in temperature or when water gets supersaturated with oxygen.

Symptoms

Fishes swim at an angle of 45° with head pointing down. In older fishes bubbles can be observed in the eyes, gills, skin and mouth. Darker colour and blindness occurs due to the presence of bubble in eye.

Treatment

Fishes should be immediately transferred to other ponds which have healthy and adequate water quality. In an intensive culture system, leakage in pump and valve should be checked.

Disorders

Many types of domestic and industrial pollutants which enter the water body affect the fish stock directly and results in many disorders.

(a) Chlorine (Cl)

Causative factor

Presence of chlorine above 4 mg l^{-1} of water create disorders in fish.

Symptoms

Anaemic and fading of body (anaemic and discoloured) results in death after 8 h, in most of the carp species.

(b) Ammonia

Causative factor : Presence of Ammonia above 1 mg l^{-1} of water results in various disorders

Symptoms : External bleeding

(c) Hydrogen sulphide

Causative factor : Presence of hydrogen sulphide above 0.6 mg l^{-1}.

Symptoms : The gills becoming reddish violet in colour.

(d) Acidosis

Causative factors : Due to the acid rains, when the pH of water becomes acidic.

Symptoms : Fish show abnormal and very fast swimming and jumping behaviour, dark greyish deposits on the body, darkening of the edges and mucous secretion can be observed.

Treatment : Balance the pH value by adding powdered calcium carbonate.

(e) Alkalosis

Causative factor : Excesssive alkaline condition (higher pH value)

Symptoms : Fish show abnormal and very fast swimming behaviour

Treatment : By buffering the medium and suitable calcification

Several other substances which create disorders in fishes are phenols, synthetic detergents, alkalies, arsenic salts, manganese chloride, acids, iron, nitrate and carbon-di-oxide etc.

Environment related diseases/disorders

Fish is an aquatic vertebrate and is very sensitive to environmental changes. Therefore, physico-chemical characteristics of water are of great importance in fish culture, their survival and growth.

Lack of oxyen

- The oxygen requirement of fishes varies from species to species and carps normally needs 6 to 7 mg l^{-1} of oxygen at 20°C.
- Oxygen deficiency causes suffocation and fish mortality may occur immediately.

Temperture variations

- Extremes of temperatures (higher or lower) are harmful for the survival of fishes. A suitable temperature for carps is about 20 to 37°C.

(j) NUTRITIONAL DEFICIENCY DISEASES

(a)	**Name of the disease**	:	Pin head
	Causative factor	:	Starvation or underfeeding
	Symptoms	:	Observe enlarged head and slender body
	Treatment	:	Provide balanced adequate diet
(b)	**Name of the disease**	:	Lipoid hepatic degeneration
	Causative factor	:	Over feeding
	Symptoms	:	Anaemia follows with gills looking pale
	Treatment	:	Stop feeding
(c)	**Causative factor**	:	Vitamin E. deficiency
	Symptoms	:	Deformation of body and fins
	Treatment	:	By feeding nutrionally balanced diet containing vitamin E.
(d)	**Causative factor**	:	Deficiency of potassium Iodide (KI)
	Symptoms	:	Observe thyroid tumours
	Treatment	:	By feeding on nutritionally balanced diet containing adequate amount of iodine
(e)	**Causative factor**	:	Vitamin A
	Symptoms	:	Excess of Vitamin A leads to squamous metaplasia, splenomegaly and hepatomegaly **(deficiency hypo vitamin A)** Under growth, blindness, haemorrhage at the fin base and keratomalacia.
(f)	**Causative factor**	:	**Vitamin B_6 deficiency**

	Symptoms	:	Fish show nervous signs and gasping of the opercular folds etc.
(g)	**Name of the disease**	:	Nutritional gill disease
	Causative factor	:	Pantothenic acid deficiency
	Symptoms	:	Secondary gill lamellae are clubbed, primary gill lamellae shows hyperplasia, Inappetence, respiratory troubles and anaemia.
(h)	**Causative factor**	:	Deficiency of Vitamin C
	Symptoms	:	Observe poor wound healing (recovery), abnormal skeletal development.

TREATMENT PROCEDURES

Immersion Treatments

(a) Bath treatment
(b) Dip treatment
(c) Prolonged immersion
(d) Flushes
(e) Flowing treatment

(a) Bath treatment

Bathing the animal/fish *in situ* in a chemial solution for 30-60 minutes is called as bath treatment.

(b) Dip treatment

Dipping the fish in a solution of high concentration for 1-5 minutes is known as dip treatment.

(c) Prolonged immersion

Bathing the fish *in situ* in solutions of low concentration for a period exceeding 12h is known as prolonged immersion treatment.

(d) Flushes

When a small volume of the concentrated chemical is added to the in-flow water holding fishes is called flush treatment.

(e) Flowing treatment

When a constant volume of the chemical is added in the inflowing water current over a fixed time to achieve a required concentration is called flowing treatment.

Exercise 1 : Collect and identify common fish parasites and draw diagrams.

Exercise 2 : Identify the disease/s from the infected fish specimen.

CHAPTER **6**

Fish Physiology and Behaviour

Experiment 6.1 **:** *Estimation of RBC present in cubic mm volume of blood.*

Instrument

Haemocytometer

Materials

(i) Blood sample

(ii) Microscope

(iii) Hayan's solution

(iv) Prickling needle

Structure of Haemocytometer

(i) Glass slide

(ii) Central 'H' shaped chamber

(iii) 2 prominent ridges, each ridge with 5 cubical chambers, each cubical chamber further sub-divided into 25 sub-divisions

- 4 side cubical chambers each with 16 sub-divisions
- Total division in central chamber are $(25 \times 16 = 400)$
- Central chamber is used to count RBC or WBC
- Haemocytometer includes a pipette

HAYAN'S SOLUTION

It contains

(i)	Mercuric chloride ($HgCl_2$)	=	0.5 g
(ii)	Sodium chloride (NaCl)	=	1.0 g
(iii)	Sodium sulphate (Na_2SO_4)	=	5.00 g
(iv)	Distilled water (H_2O)	=	200 ml

$HgCl_2$ acts as a corrosive sublimate and fixes the RBC's in the blood. The other ingredients acts isotonically so that RBC's may not burst due to haémolysis. Hayan's solution also serve to dilute the blood.

Procedure

- Clean and dry mixing pipette (dilution 1:2000).
- Take the fish in hand and cut the tail so that blood flows freely. If necessary sqeeze it.

Note : *Leave the first few drops to flow away*

- Suck blood with RBC pipette upto the 0.5 mark slowly and carefully.
- Wipe the tip of the pipette.
- Suck Hayan's diluting fluid upto 101 mark (Hayan's fluid prevent haemolysis, coagulation and bacterial growth).
- Mix and shake thoroughly for a minute.
- Transfer the blood onto the counting chamber covered with a cover glass.
- Avoid the overflow of mixture from the chamber and trapping of air bubbles.
- Allow the cells to settle.
- Bring counting scale into the focus under a microscope.

Counting

Select smaller squares for counting, taking one from each four corners and fifth one from the centre.

Calculation

$$\text{No. of RBC/cubic mm} = \frac{\text{No. of RBC counted} \times \text{Dilution} \times \text{Depth}}{\text{Area of chamber counted}}$$

Depth of chamber = 0.1 mm

Dilution of blood = 200 times and

Area counted is 80/400 = 1/5 sq mm

$$= \frac{\text{Number of RBC counted} \times 200 \times 10}{1/5}$$

$$= \text{Number of RBC counted} \times 10{,}000$$

Experiment 6.2 **:** *Determination of haemoglobin contents of fish blood.*

Fish is an aquatic vertebrate and its blood is liable to be affected by a variety of substances occurring in the media, therefore, measurement of haemoglobin contents will yield a lot of information about the environment, pathological conditions and physiological state of the fish. Haemoglobin (Hb) is present in the erythrocytes and is a principal oxygen carrier substance.

Materials

(i) Haemoglobinometer

(ii) Live fish

Procedure

- Fill the central diluting tube with 20 cu mm of N/10 HCl (9 ml of HCl in 1 L of distilled water).
- Bleed the fish and suck 20 cu mm of blood in a pipette/capillary.
- Transfer the blood by blowing the pipette/capillary gently in the diluting tube and rinse the capillary several times so that no trace of blood is left in it.
- After about 10 minutes add drop by drop distilled water or N/10 HCl with continuous stirring till the colour of blood in the diluting tube start matching with the standard tubes.
- Record the dilution of the blood and also note the point where its colour matches with the colour of the standard tube and calculate haemoglobin as mg ml^{-1} of blood.

Experiment 6.3 : Determination of methaemoglobin percentage from fish blood.

Addition of fertilizers, decaying organic matter, sewage and domestic effluents, industrial discharges in the aquatic environment contribute largely to an increase in nitrite (NO_2) concentrations. Nitrite toxicity results in the change of oxygen carrying capacity of the blood by converting haemoglobin to methaemoglobin and thus the demand for oxygen increases in the animals exposed to such aquatic environments. Therefore, measurement of methaemoglobin from the blood could indicate the extent of nitrite toxicity.

Principle

Ferricyanide converts haemoglobin iron from ferrous to ferric to form methaemoglobin, which combine with potassium cyanide to form a stable pigment known as cynmethaemoglobin.

Thus methaemoglobin is measured as cynmethaemoglobin.

Preparation of a calibration curve

Prepare a Drabkin's diluent solution as follows :

1. Sodium bi-carbonate ($NaHCO_3$) 1.0 g
2. Potassium ferricynide (K_3 $Fe(CN)_6$) 200 mg
3. Potassium cyanide (KCN) 50 mg

Make the volume to 1000 ml by adding distilled water :

- Obtain following dilutions of Drabkin's diluent by mixing it with ortho-Acuglobin

	O-Acuglobin Haemoglobin		Drabkin's solution	Dilution
1.	1	:	3	25
2.	1	:	1	50
3.	3	:	1	75

Materials required

(i) Live fish

(ii) Chemicals (Drabkin diluent solution, 0-acuglobin).

Procedure

- Set zero of the spectrophotometer using distilled water or Drabkin's solution.
- Take 5 ml of Drabkin's diluent solution in a cuvette.
- Add 20 μl of blood with capillary and rinse the capillary atleast 3-4 times with the diluent.
- Vortex for 10 minutes, read OD at 540 nm.
- Calculate the concentration from the standard curve.

Experiment 6.4 : *Determination of plasma calcium.*

Plasma calcium can be measured using murexide technique (Snell, 1978).

Materials required

(i) Blood plasma

(ii) *Working reagent : Murexide 80 mg l^{-1} in propylen^ glycol + 30 ml of 3.75 N KOH l^{-1}

(iii) Calcium carbonate

(iv) Spectrophotometer

Procedure

- Take 50 μl of plasma, dilute it to 2.5 ml with distilled water and mix 1.5 ml of working reagent*.
- Read the absorbance against a blank at 490 nm.

Prepare a calcium standard curve using solutions of high quality (BDH or E merck) calcium carbonate in double distilled deionised water.

Standard curve

- Dissolve 250.0 mg $CaCO_3$ in 1L deionised double distilled water. 1 ml of this solution will contain 100 μg of calcium. Prepare other standards as follows :

	Standard solution (100 μg/ml)	Distilled water	Final concentration (μg/ml)
1.	50 ml	0.0 ml	100 μg
2.	40 ml	10.0 ml	80 μg
3.	30 ml	20.0 ml	60 μg
4.	20 ml	30.0 ml	40 μg
5.	10 ml	40.0 ml	20 μg
6.	0.0 ml	50.0 ml	0.0μg

Take the absorbance at 490 nm and plot a standard curve between absorbance and concentration.

Experiment 6.5 : *Determination of steroids from a given sample by thin layer chromatography (TLC)*

Materials required

(i) Silica Gel-G
(ii) Activated TLC plate (20 cm× 20cm) and TLC chamber
(iii) Chloroform
(iv) Acetone
(v) Steroid samples
(vi) Iodine crystals
(vii) Incubator

Procedure

- Make a slurry of silica gel-G by mixing it with distilled water (1:2).
- Take the TLC plate and spread a 0.25 mm thick layer of silica Gel-G slurry using a thick glass rod or spreader.
- Dry the plate at room temperature and activate at 110°C for 45 min before use.
- Take out the plate, when cool, draw a base line on the TLC plate at a distance of about 3.5 cm from one end of the plate.
- Meanwhile prepare a chromatographic chamber by pouring a mixture of chloroform and acetone (9:1) so that the chamber gets saturated.
- Apply the reference solution (maximum 10 μl) and other steroids on the base line using glass capillaries/micro pipette/lambda pipette.
- Apply the solutions in small lots with drying in between so that the spot size does not increase beyond 0.5 cm diameter.
- Place the TLC plate in the chamber so that the baseline end dips in the mobile phase and the other rests against the wall of the chamber.

- Leave the chamber undisturbed and allow the mobile phase to travel about 2/3rd length of the plate.
- Remove the plate and measure the distance travelled by the solvent front (mobile phase) from the baseline.
- Then develop the plate by keeping it in another chamber already saturated with iodine (by keeping iodine crystals).
- Encircle the spots saturated with iodine.
- Measure the distance travelled by the spots/samples fronts from the baseline.

$$Rf = \frac{\text{Distance travelled by the steroids (sample)}}{\text{Distance travelled by the solvent front}}$$

Rf is characteristic of every given compound.

Experiment 6.6 : *Determination of the effects of Gonadotropins-GtH (FSH, LH) on fish gonads during the non-breeding period.*

Materials

(i) Live fish specimens

(ii) Gonadotropins (FSH and LH)

(iii) 0.64% NaCl solution

Procedure

- Obtain about 30 specimens of fish (preferably a catfish), divide into three groups of ten fishes each and allocate them to three different aquaria.
- Inject FSH or LH (@ LH 10-25 μg Kg^{-1} BW or FSH-100 μg Kg^{-1} BW d^{-1} to one group daily for 10 to 15 days.
- Give saline injections to the third group daily.
- At the end of the treatment, remove fish one by one from each treatment, weigh them individually, dissect and record GSI (calculate mean and compare the two means by applying students 't' test). Note gonadal recrudescence in GtH treated fishes.

Note : *Give intramascular injections.*

- Keep the volume injected constant (say 0.5 ml/fish/day).

Experiment 6.7 : *Demonstrate the digestive processes in a given fish by showing the presence of trypsin, Amylase and lipase.*

Materials

(i) Glycerine

(ii) Toluene

(iii) Glass stoppered bottle

(iv) Live fish

Procedure

- Cut open the belly of the freshly killed fish.
- Remove the small intestine.
- Give a length wise cut to the intestine and wash its contents using distilled water.
- Place the intestine in the grinder containing 20 ml of 50% glycerine. Grind the tissue and decant the liquid in a separate beaker.
- Add another 20 ml of 50% glycerine and grind it again till a suspension of fine particles in the glycerol is obtained.
- Add toluene (in excess) to it and store the contents in a glass stoppered amber coloured bottle at room temperature.
- After four days, filter the solution and use it for the determination of enzymes (Trypsin, Amylase and Lipase) as follows :

Trypsin

Take four glass tubes.

Ist tube

Add 5 ml of sodium carbonate solution (1%) + white of an egg.

2nd tube

Take 5 ml of sodium carbonate solution (1%) + a little of boiled intestinal extract + white of an egg.

3rd tube

Take 5 ml of sodium carbonate solution (1%) and a little of intestinal extract (not boiled) + white of an egg.

4th tube

Take 5 ml of 1 N HCl and a little of intestinal extract + white of an egg

- Keep all the four tubes for 1/2h in a water bath maintained at 40°C and test the contents for the presence of peptones (trypsin converts proteins into peptones) with biuret test as follows :
- Add five drops of copper sulphate solution (10g l^{-1}) to 2 ml of the test solution followed by 2 ml of NaOH solution (10 mol/l) in each test tube, mix thoroughly, and note the change in colour to violet.

Note : *Colour (violet) change (positive biuret test) is seen in test tube No. 3 only indicating that boiling and addition of HCl denatures the enzyme.*

Amylase

- Take a thin starch paste in a glass tube.
- Add to it a little of intestinal extract.
- Keep the test-tube for 30 minutes in a water bath maintained at 40°C.
- Test the contents of the tube for the presence of
  - (i) sugars with Benedict's reagent
  - (ii) starch by adding few drops of iodine solution
- With benedict's reagent, contents will show positive test indicating the presence of sugar.
- Addition of iodine solutions shows negative test for starch indicating that the starch has been changed into sugar under the influence of the amylase.

Lipase

- Prepare an emulsion by adding a few drops of olive oil in 10 ml of water and 2 ml of soap solution.
- Shake the contents and divide the emulsion into two test tubes.
- Add a few drops of intestinal extract in both the tubes.
- Boil the contents of one of the test tube and place both the tubes in an incubator maintained at 37°C for 24 hours.
- Test the solutions in the test tubes with litmus paper.
- Note the change in colour of litmus paper in both the test tubes.

Note : (i) *Boiling denature's the enzyme creating alkaline medium which changes red litmus to blue.*

(ii) In the second tube blue litmus is changed to red because of the acidic medium due to the presence of active enzyme.

Experiment 6.8 : *To study colour change in fish skin.*

Requirements

(i) 0.6% NaCl

(ii) Dissecting instruments

(iii) Microscope

(iv) White enamel bowl

(v) Fish

Pigments of different colours are usually present in the skin, in cells called chromatophores. These cells commonly contain a black or brown pigment called melanine and are called melanocytes. Yellow (xanthine) and red (carotene) pigments also occur in the skin of vertebrates and are contained in chromatophores called xanthophores and erythrophores respectively. Some chromatophore containing pteridine platelets, which give an iridiscent appearance, are called iridophores.

Many vertebrates can change their colouration in response to environmental and behavioural needs. The cold blooded vertebrates like frogs can change their body colour rapidly i.e. it takes a few minutes to few hours. This relatively rapid response is called physiological colour change. These colour changes are influenced by the actions of hormones from the pituitary (Melanocyte stimulating hormone-MSH).

There are five distinct stages representing different degree of pigment dispersion within the chromatophores. Most aggregated stage is designated as 1, and most dispersed as 5 (See fig. 6.1). Calculate the Melanophore index as follows.

Melanophore index × (MI) = No. of chromatophores in particular stage × particular stage number

Procedure

- Expose the animals to different light regimes (continuous light, continuous dark) and different backgrounds (such as light background, dark background and coloured background) for 24 hours.
- After 24 hours take a piece of skin from each fish/animal and observe the different dispersion states of chromatophores (See Fig. 6.1).

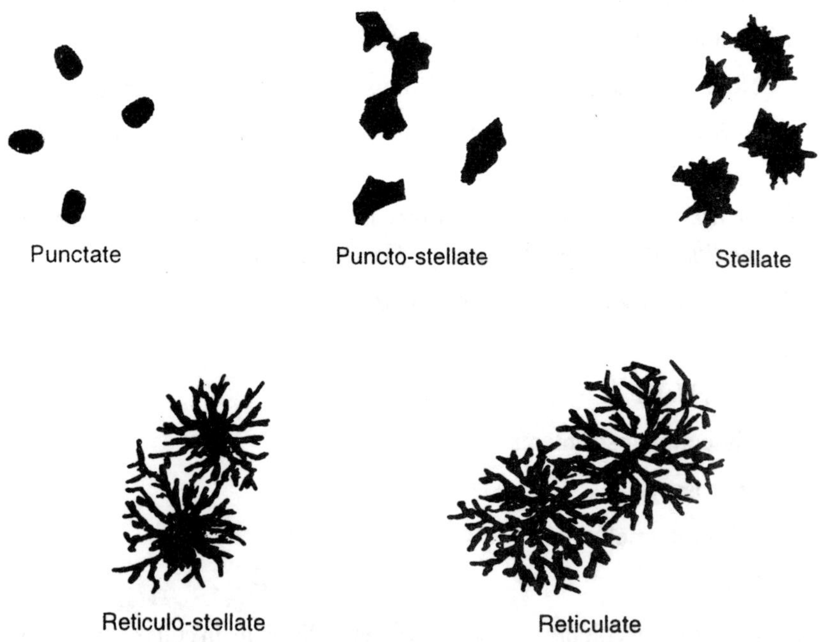

Fig. 6.1. Different stages of chromatophores (Hogben's index). The figures are numbered to demonstrate the index.

- Record details as given in Table 14.
- Calculate the melanophore index (Hogben's index).
- Also study the effect of blinding and melatonin injection/pineal extract on melanophore index.

Table 14 :

Observation : Normal and AP fishes adapted to dark background

Stages	MI* in AP fish		MI in normal fish		Mean MI for AP fish	Mean MI for normal fish
	Chromatophore No.	Chromatophore Nos.×stage No (MI)	Chromatophores No.	Chromatophore Nos.× stage No. (MI)		
1.						
2.						
3.						
4.						
5.						

*MI = Melanophore index
AP = Hypophysectomized fish

Experiment 6.9 : To study the rate of respiration.

Principle

Depending upon the environmental temperature the rate of respiration is accelerated or retarded. This is clearly reflected on opercular movements also.

Procedure

- Take a water bath. Fill it half with water and note the temperature.
- Release a fish and note the number of opercular movements per minute.
- Raise the temperature to 10°C and again note the number of opercular movements. In this way the experiment can be repeated at 3-4 different temperatures.

Note : *Observe an increase in the number of opercular movements with increase in water temperature.*

Experiment 6.10 : *To study temperature preference of Channa **punctatus/common carp/ Heteropneustes fossilis/or any other Indian major carp species.***

Materials

(i) Rectangular wooden box, Thermometers (six), fish, ice, polythene bags.

Procedure

- Take a glass aquarium/wooden box (Fig. 6.2)
- Partition it into five equal chambers using asbestos' sheets.

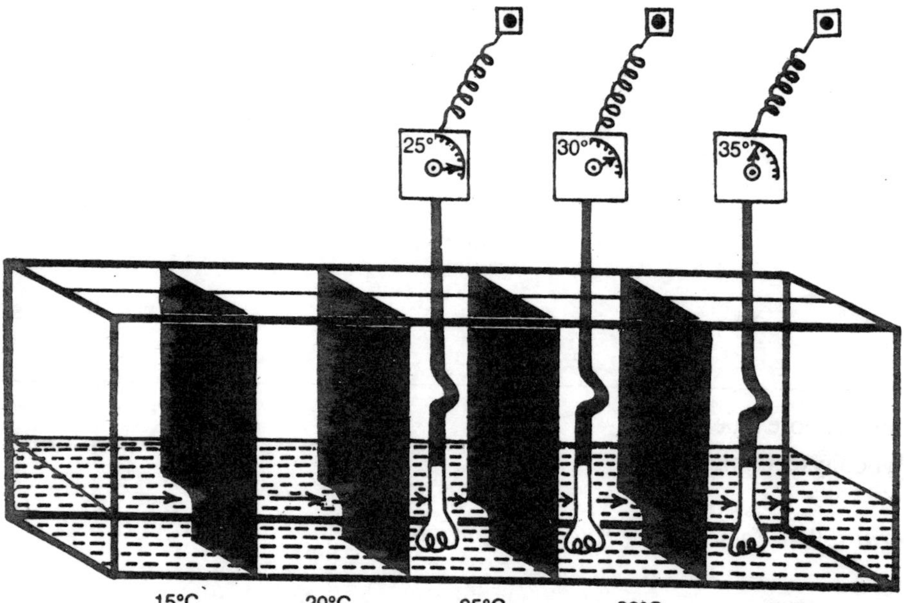

Fig. 6.2. Glass aquarium/wooden box partitioned into five equal chambers for creating a thermal gradient from 15° to 35°C for conducting temperature preference studies.

- Create a thermal gradient from 15-35°C.
- Maintain 15°C and 20°C by immersing ice packed polythene bags.
- For maintaining 25°, 30° and 35°C, use thermostatically controlled water heaters.
- Release a group of about 10 fish and keep noting the water temperature of the spot, where each fish settles at periodical intervals.
- At the end of experiment (about 2 h), calculate the weighted average for each time point.

Experiment 6.11 : *To study temperature tolerance of Channa punctatus/common carp/ Heteropneustes fossilis/or any other Indian major carp species.*

Materials

(i) Fish
(ii) Thermometer, aquaria, water bath, ice packets

Procedure

Minimal lethal temperature

- Take water in aquaria, release a group of about 10 fish in it and record the temperature.
- Gradually cool the water by immersing ice packed polythene bags.
- Temperature may be lowered at the rate of 1-3°C/h.
- Record the temperature when a fish dies. Continue lowering the temperature till all fish dies.

Maximal lethal temperature

- Release a group of about 10 fish in a water bath and gradually raise the temperature.
- Record the temperature when a fish dies. Continue raising the temperature till all fish dies.
- Plot the graph and calculate minimal lethal and maximal lethal temperatures.

Experiment 6.12 : *To study salinity tolerance in a fresh water carp/or in an air breathing fish.*

Fishes thrive both in fresh water and seawater and are able to regulate ionic concentrations of their internal body fluids. Two types of fish viz. Stenohaline and Euryhaline can be distinguished regarding salinity tolerance. Euryhaline fishes have wide tolerance range while stenohaline fishes have narrow tolerance limits.

Materials

(i) Fish
(ii) Glass aquaria, measuring cylinder
(iii) Chemicals required for preparing sea water

Procedure

- Take 9 aquarias of 10 L capacity each.
- Prepare dilutions of seawater* (100%, 80%, 60%, 50%, 40%, 30%, 20%, 10%) and use freshwater as control. Add 5L of each dilution in each aquarium.
- Release 5-7 fish in each aquarium and make observations after 24h, 48h, 72h, 7 days, 9 days, 12 days and 15 days and record observations in the following table:

Table 15. *Observation table to record per cent mortality*

Medium (SW) (%)	No.. of fish	Per cent mortality at						
		24h	48h	72h	7 days	9 days	12 days	15 days
100								
80								
60								
50								
40								
30								
20								
10								
Fresh water								

*Preparation of full strength sea water (SW)

		g/l
1.	Sodium chloride (NaCl)	23.4
2.	Potassium chloride (KCl)	0.73
3.	Calcium chloride ($CaCl_2$)	1.12
4.	Magnesium chloride ($MgCl_2.6H_2O$)	10.71
5.	Sodium sulphate (Na_2SO_4)	3.94
6.	Sodium bicarbonate ($NaHCO_3$)	0.21
7.	Sodium bromide (NaBr)	0.06

Exercise 1: Compare the melanophore index of pinealectomized fish with those of normal fish.

Exercise 2 : Compare the melanophore indices of dark background adapted and light background adapted fish.

Exercise 3 : Study the effect of melatonin and epinephrine on melanophore index and compare your results with fish injected with saline solution.

Exercise 4 : Study the effect of salinity, temperature and epinephrine on rate of respiration and oxygen consumption.

CHAPTER 7

Fish Reproduction and Breeding

Experiment 7.1 : *Determination of Gonosomatic Index (GSI) of given fishes.*

The most common means of accounting for the effects of differential body size on gonad size (to normalize gonad size) is to express gonadal weight as a percentage of body weight. The ratio (gonadal weight/body weight) multiplied by 100 is termed as gonosomatic index or GSI.

Materials

(i) Fish, anaesthesia, balance

Procedure

- Take the fish and wipe it dry with cloth napkin/cheese cloth.
- Record the weight on a top pan balance. (using MS 222 or any other anaesthesia).
- Anaesthesize the fish, cut upon the belly, extirpate the gonads (ovary/testes) carefully.
- Place these on a piece of tin foil and record the weight separately for male and female fish.

Calculations

$$GSI = \frac{\text{Gonadal weight}}{\text{Body weight}} \times 100$$

Experiment 7.2 : *Determination of Hepatosomatic index (HSI) of given fishes.*

Gonadal recrudescence in some female fishes involves an accumulation of lipids and protein stores within the developing oocytes. These stores comes from some visceral organs, body musculature and ingested food. Therefore, weight changes in some visceral organs such as liver may be inversely correlated with oocyte development in some species. Liver size in a sample of fishes is generally expressed as a percentage of body weight minus (-) gonad weight and expressed as hepatosomatic index or HSI.

Materials

(i) Fish, anaesthesia, balance

Procedure

- Take the fish and wipe it dry with cloth napkin/cheese cloth.
- Record the weight on a top pan balance. Anaesthesize the fish, cut upon the belly, extirpate the gonads and liver carefully.
- Place these organs on separate pieces of tin foil and record their weight separately.

Calculations

$$HSI = \frac{\text{Liver weight}}{\text{Body weight - gonad weight}} \times 100$$

Experiment 7.3 : Determination of Relative Gonadal Index (RGI).

Relative gonadal index is an alternative index for the quantification of reproductive condition. This index detects gonadal development independent of the weight of the fish and controls for allometry.

Procedure

- Record the weight of the fish.
- Dissect the fish and extirpate the ovaries.
- Blot the ovaries to dryness and weigh it.
- Calculate RGI as follows :

$$RGI = W[(S^B).10]$$

Where,

W = Ovarian weight (g)

S = Body weight - weight (g) of ovaries

B = Weighted average of statistically homogenous regression coefficients of the relationship. In (W) versus In (S) estimated separately for each ovarian development stage using analysis of covariance (ANOVA).

Experiment 7.4 : Determination of condition factor (CF) for reproductive fish.

Materials

(i) Fish, anaesthesia, balance, measuring scale

Procedure

- Weigh (g) the fish and measure its length (cm).
- Dissect it and extirpate the gonads and liver.

- Weigh the liver and gonads separately.
- Calculate CF as follows :

$$\text{Condition factor (CF)} = \frac{\text{Body Weight - (liver + gonad weight)}}{\text{length}^3} \times 100$$

Experiment 7.5* : *Determination of pituitary Somatic Index (PSI).

Weight (size) of the pituitary gland changes with change in the stage of reproductive cycle and thus is directly proportional to the weight of gonads.

Materials

(i) Fish, anaesthesia, balance, butchers knife.

Procedure

- Take the weight and kill the fish.
- Expose the skull using butchers knife.
- Carefully lift the brain holding medulla oblongata.
- Locate the pituitary lying underneath .
- Remove it carefully using a fine pair of forceps.
- Place it on a pre weighed piece of tin foil. Immediately record the weight (mg) of the pituitary along with the piece of tin foil .

$$\text{PSI} = \frac{\text{Wt. of pituitary (mg)}}{\text{Wt. of fish (g)}} \times 100$$

Experiment 7.6* : *Determination of fecundity.

The number of eggs produced per unit body weight of female fish is termed as fecundity.

Materials

(i) Weighing balance.

(ii) Gilson's fluid (100 ml 60% alcohol, 15 ml of 80% nitric acid, 18 ml of glacial acetic acid, 20g mercuric chloride 880 ml of distilled water).

(iii) Microscope

Procedure

1. - Record the weight of the fish.
   - Dissect the fish and extirpate the ovaries.
   - Take a weighed portion of the ovary and place it in the Gilson's fluid with occassional shaking to release the oocytes.
   - Take a suitable sub-sample and count the oocytes.

- The total number of oocytes in the ovaries are then estimated using the formula:

$$N = \left(\frac{V}{V'}\right) n \times \left(\frac{W}{w'}\right)$$

Where,

V = Volume of sample

V' = Volume of sub-sample

W = Weight of ovaries

W' = Weight of portion of the ovary used in sample

n = Number of oocytes in sub-sample

2. - Record the weight of fish.
- Remove the ovaries and preserve in Gilson's fluid for 3 months.
- Shake the sample periodically to ensure separation of eggs from ovarian tissue.
- After 3 months, decant the Gilson's fluid, wash and dry the sample.
- Weigh all the eggs from each fish.
- Take three random sub-samples and count the number of eggs in each sub-sample.
- Calculate fecundity as follows :

$$F = \left(\frac{Wn}{x}\right)$$

Where,

F = Total number of eggs in the ovary.

W = Weight of all the eggs from fish.

n = Number of eggs counted in the sub-sample.

x = Dry weight of sub-sample

Experiment 7.7 : Determination of percentage or rate of fertilization.

Materials

(i) Eggs from fertilization bowl/hapa.

(ii) 5% glacial Acetic acid

Procedure

- Take the sample of water hardened eggs.
- Place these in 5% glacial acetic acid for about 24 hours.
- Dead eggs will become translucent while fertilized will be transparent.

Calculate the percentage of fertilization.

$$\% \text{ fertilization} = \frac{\text{No. of fertilized eggs}}{\text{Total no. of eggs in the sample}} \times 100$$

Experiment 7.8 : *Identify and write short notes on the following :*

(a) T.S. of fish testes, (b) T.S. of fish ovary, (c) T.S. of fish Interrenal, (d) T.S. of fish thyroid, (e) Sagittal section of fish pituitary.

(a) T.S. of fish Testes

Transverse section of fish testes shows that it is composed of a large number of seminiferous tubules which are closely bound together by a thin layer of connective tissue. Following different stages are seen :

(i) ***Germ cells or primary spermatogonia*** : They occur at all times of the year. They possess a large spherical nucleus surrounded by clear cytoplasm and is the largest cell in the testes. It undergoes mitotic divisions and gives rise to secondary spermatogonia.

(ii) ***Secondary spermatogonia*** : These are smaller in size and have a dark spherical nucleus with chromatin mass. It gives rise to primary and secondary spermatocytes.

(iii) ***Primary and secondary spermatocytes*** : Primary spermatocytes are morphologically similar to secondary spermatocyte. They possess a dark nucleus with a thin rim of cytoplasm. They quickly increase in size, however, their spherical nuclei are usually seen in the prophase of the first meiotic division. The secondary spermatocytes are smaller than the primary spermatocytes and have smaller nuclei. Their period of existence is short. They divide meiotically and give rise to spermatids.

(iv) ***Spermatids*** : They are compact dot like structures with haploid nucleus. They are situated near the lumen of the tubule.

(v) ***Spermatozoa*** : Spermatids metamorphosed into spermatozoans. Small spermatozoans or sperms are seen filling the lumen of seminiferous tubules.

(b) T.S. of fish ovary (Fig. 7.1)

Examine the following three stages of oocytes in the stained ovarian sections :

(i) **Stage I : Primary Oocyte -** The non-yolky oocytes present in the ovary during all seasons of the year.

(ii) **Stage II : Primacy Oocytes -** These are characterized by the presence of a ring of cortical alveoli an indication of the onset of vitellogenesis.

(iii) **Stage III : Primary Oecytes -** These are fully formed yolky oocytes seen in the ovary only during the breeding period.

Examine the structure of the ovarian wall consisting of many follicular layers.

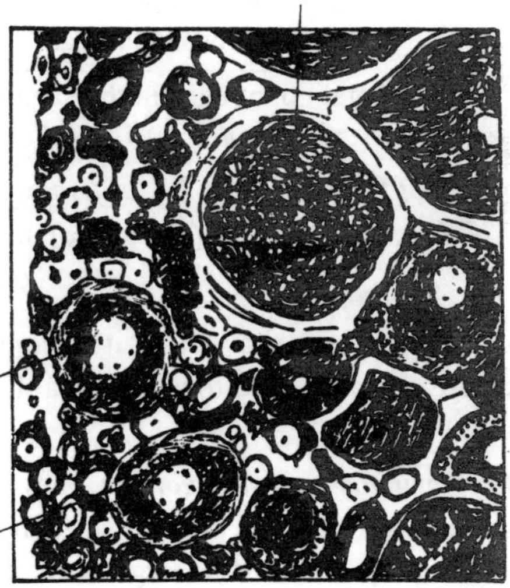

Fig. 7.1. T.S. of fish ovary (Stage I primary oocytes, stage II vitellogenic oocytes, stage III yolky oocytes).

(c) T.S. of fish interrenal

In fishes interrenal tissue (adrenal) is present in the two lobes of the head kidney which are situated anterior to the main kidneys. Interrenal tissue is arranged in the form of cords of cells around the lumen of the posterior cardinal veins and is surrounded externally by haemopoietic tissue. Posterior cardinal vein passes through the head kidney. Histologically the cortical and the medullary cells (chromaffin) exists together and no particular distribution pattern is evident.

In the non-breeding period

- Size of the interrenal tissue is small.
- Cords of cells around the lumen are few.
- Haemopoietic tissue abundant.
- Nuclei of the cortical cells show an irregular outline and granular cytoplasm.
- Chromaffin cells few.

During the breeding period

- Interrenal cells get hypertrophied often as many as 100 layers of cells can be seen.
- Haemopoietic tissue gets reduced in size.
- Chromaffin cells also increase in number.

(d) T.S. of fish thyroid

The thyroid gland as in most of the bony fishes is an unencapsulated structure and consist of a large number of follicles, which are irregularly distributed around the ventral arotea up to the mid end of the afferent branchial artery arising from the ventral arota. A transverse section passing through ventral arota clearly shows the thyroid follicles interspersed with the connective tisue fibres.

- The follicles consists of similar layer of cuboidal epithelium which becomes columnar.
- Thyroid follicles gradually increase in number and surface area with the approach of the breeding period.
- Follicles which were empty in the regressed fish are seen to be filled with colloid.
- An increase in the number of follicles occurs.
- Epithelial lining gradually becomes columnar, nuclei becomes large and elongated. Lumen appear larger and becomes full of colloids.

(e) Sagittal Section of fish pituitary (Fig. 7.2)

Description pertains to the sagittal section of Indian catfish *Heteropneustes fossilis*.

Following three regions characteristic of teleosts pituitary are seen :

1. Rostral pars distalis (RPD)
2. Proximal pars distalis (PPD)
3. Pars intermedia (PI)

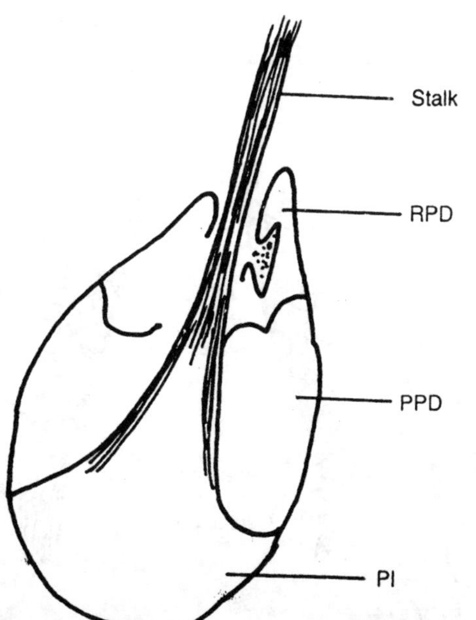

Fig. 7.2. Sagittal section (diagrammatic) of fish pituitary (RPD-rostral pars distalis, PPD-proximal pars distalis, PI-pars intermedia).

The pituitary is seen connected to the hypothalamus by a solid stalk of nerve fibres forming the central core of pituitary gland. It branches and innervates the three regions of pituitary gland. No clear demarcation between adenohypophysis and neurohypophysis are seen. Numerous blood vessels are seen in the Pars Nervosa. The three different regions of pituitary are seen containing different types of secretary cells responsible for secreting different types of pituitary hormones.

Experiment 7.9 **:** *Determination of Oocytes diameter.*

Oocyte diameter can be measured by a calibrated eye piece using only spherical oocytes cut through the nucleus. For mean ova diameter, atleast 50 oocytes selected at random from each sample must be measured.

- Ova diameter can also be measured using a graduated microscope or projection microscope which has been standardized using a micrometer.
- Oocyte diameter should be taken from the longest axis of the oocyte.
- Measurements be made only from such oocytes which are not deformed.

Experiment 7.10 **:** *To identify male and female brood fish in (a) Common carp (Cyprinus carpio) and (b) Indian major carps*

(a) Common carp, ***Cyprinus carpio***

Common carp shows sexual dimorphism and thus can be easily identified by looking at the following characters of the male and female (See fig. 7.3) spawners/fish.

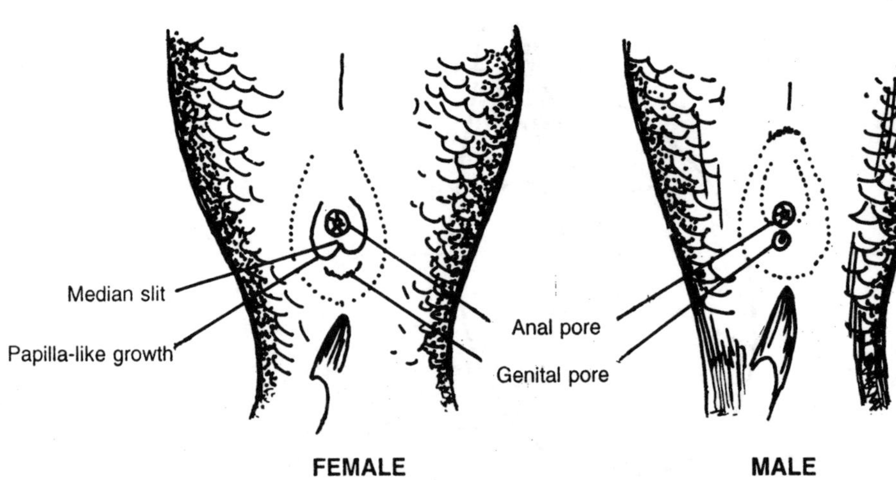

Fig. 7.3. Sexual dimorphism in common carp.

	Female	Male
(i)	The reddish vent projects like a small papilla with a narrow medium slit	Vent not projecting and the vent is like a deep pit
(ii)	When pressed eggs tend to come out	When pressed gently milk oozes out
(iii)	Smooth dorsal surface of pectoral fin	Rough dorsal surface of the pectoral fin
(iv)	Body smooth and slimy	Body rough to touch
(v)	Abdomen large swollen and bulging	Not so large

(b) Indian major carps

They do not show any sexual dimorphism, therefore, it is difficult to distinguish the males and females during the non-breeding period. However, during spawning season males and females can be distinguished as follows :

	Female	Male
(i)	Eggs can be seen on pressing the belly	Ripe males oozes milt freely on gently pressing the abdomen
(ii)	The abdomen is soft, bulging and rounded, vent is reddish	Not so bulging and vent not so red
(iii)	Note smooth dorsal surface of the pectoral fin	Rough dorsal surface of the pectoral fin

(c) Catfishes like *Heteropneustes fossilis, Aorichthys seenghala* or *Clarias batrachus* etc. also show sexual dimorphism and the males can be easily distinguished from the females by the presence of a small genital papilla, while the female has a slit like opening in the vent region.

***Experiment 7.11* : *Breeding of common carp, Cyprinus carpio*.**

Common carp breeds almost throughout the year, even in stagnant/confined waters. However, 2-3 (February-March, September-October) major peaks can be observed during its reproductive cyclicity and no hormonal injections are normally required to breed the fish.

Methodology

- Seggregate the male and female brooders a few months/(2-3 months) prior to the breeding season.
- Stock the brood fish (male and female) in separate ponds (which are free from other fishes).
- Feed the brood fish on a mixtore of oilcake and rice bran (1:1) @ 2-3% of their body weight.
- If there is any algal bloom in the ponds suspend feeding immediately, while keeping a watch on the health of the breeders.
- Breed the fish as follows :

(a) Hapa breeding

- Fix the hapa in the ponds with the help of four bamboo sticks (See fig. 7.4).
- Introduce common submerged aquatic weeds like *Hydrilla*, najas, potomogeton @ 2 kg of weeds per one kg of the weight of the female fish as egg stickers.
- Release the brood fish in the hapa preferably in the evenings (1 female and 2 or 3 males), keeping the total weight of males almost equal to tne females.
- Observe spawning in the next morning.
- Remove the brooders.
- If you want to record the fecundity, take the weight of the fish before releasing for spawning and after spawning. Record the differences in weight.
- Differentiate between the viable (fertilized) eggs from the dead ones. Dead eggs are opaque while fertilized eggs are transparent. Prepare details as given in Table 16.
- Instead of hapas, cement cisterns can also be employed for breeding purposes.

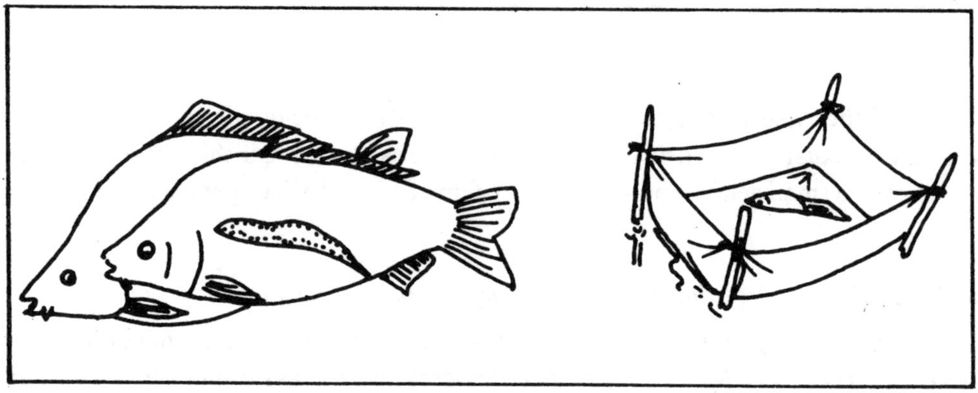

Fig. 7.4. Breeding hapa.

TABLE 10

MONITORING INDEX FOR EGG QUALITY CONTROL

DATE : Fish/species

Total weight of eggs laid	**Time/date of spawning**	No. of unfertilized/ opaque eggs	No. of normal hatchlings	No. of deformed/dead hatching	% hatchability	% survival

(b) Pond breeding

Breeding can also be done in ponds by providing bundles of the aquatic weeds.

Make strings of weeds by tieing with ropes. You can give any shape.

***Experiment 7.12** : Breeding in Indian major carp by hypophysation technique.*

Indian major carp spawn only during monsoon season and in the running water of the rivers and streams. They do not spawn in stagnant water or under laboratory conditions. They readily spawn following administration of crude pituitary extract or purified or partially purified protein hormones. Therefore, these fishes are also called difficult to spawn fishes.

(a) Induced breeding using pituitary injections

Houssay (1931) was the first scientist to describe this method.

Materials

(i) Brood fish/spawners

(ii) Pituitary glands/ovaprim.

Procedure

- A few months before the onset of spawning season, male and female breeders are sorted out and stocked separately in fertilized ponds @ 1000-2000 ha^{-1}.
- Feed the fish on groundnut oilcake and rice bran (1:1) @ 1-2% of total body weight.
- Select the fish (Indian major carp) weighing 1.5-5.0 kg, identify the sexes (as described earlier).
- Handle the breeders carefully. Selected breeders are collected with handnets and weighed individually for calculating the doses of pituitary extract (PE).
- Take out few eggs from the female brood fish using a catheter. Dip the eggs in a solution of acetic acid (70%) and alcohol (30%) for five minutes. Observe the nucleus under the microscope, if the nucleus is in the centre, fish is ready for spawning.
- Inject the pituitary extract intramuscularly at any of the sides of the brood fish such as the base of pectoral fin, axil of the pelvic fin, below the dorsal or below the lateral line or caudal peduncle.
- Give two injections (a preparatory or provocative dose @ 2-3 mg kg^{-1} and second injection or resolving dose @ 5-8 mg kg^{-1} body weight four hours after the first injection) to females.
- Give only a single dose of 2-3 mg kg^{-1} of body weight to the male fish at the time of second dose to females.
- Record the details of induced breeding as per Table 17.

TABLE 17
WORKSHEET FOR INDUCED BREEDING OF CARP

DATE : Name/species

Pond No.	Initial weight of male	Initial weight of female	Dosage of PIT extract/ ovaprim	Volume injected to each sex	Time of Ist injection	Time of IInd injection	Weight of male/ female fish after spawning	Amount of eggs	No. of eggs/ g

- After injections, introduce the male and female breeders into a breeding hapa (in the ratio of 2:1) fixed in the pond with the help of bamboo poles.
- Observe the sexual play of the breeders.
- Spawning is normally, observed after 3-6 h which is influenced by low temperature, rain water, slight drizzling and cool weather.
- If spawning doesn't occur within 3-6 h give a third injection of higher dose to the female breeders.
- Observe transparent and non-adhesive eggs of about 3-5 mm in diameter.

(b) Induced breeding using ovaprim

Ovaprim is a spawning hormone. Each ml of ovaprim contains 20 μg of Salmon GtHRH and 10 mg of domperidone.

- Take out few eggs from the female brood fish using a catheter and dip the eggs in a solution of 70% acetic acid + 30% alcohol for five minutes.
- Observe the nucleus under the microscope, if the nucleus is not in the centre the fish is not ready for spawning.
- Give only one injection simultaneously to the male and female fish.
- For females of Indian major carps 0.25 to 0.5 ml kg^{-1} body weight and for males 0.1 to 0.2 ml kg^{-1} BW gives good results.

***Experiment 7.13** : Observe different stages in the development of carp embryo.*

Stages in the development of carp egg

A carp egg : Carp eggs are demersal. Except common carp, the eggs of Indian and other exotic carps are non-adhesive. The outermost envelope of the ovulated egg is known as chorion while nucleus is covered by vitelline membrane. The space between vitelline membrane and chorion is known as peri vitelline space. The eggs imbibes water in this space and swells up during early phase of development. Depending upon the ambient temperature fertilized eggs starts developing immediately and they pass through various stages such as morula, blastula, gastrula and eyed stage (twitching stage) and hatches out as a yolk sac larva (See fig. 7.5).

***Experiment 7.14** : Visit to a fish breeding farm and to study the various components of a fish hatchery.*

Hatchery facilities are required for spawning, egg incubation, hatching and rearing upto post larval stage. The eco-hatchery system is based on chinese hatchery made to suit agroclimatic conditions of a region and water quality characteristics.

Following components make an Eco-hatchery facilities :

(a) Overhead tank

Overhead tank (OHT) is generally made of cement with sufficient water holding capacity.

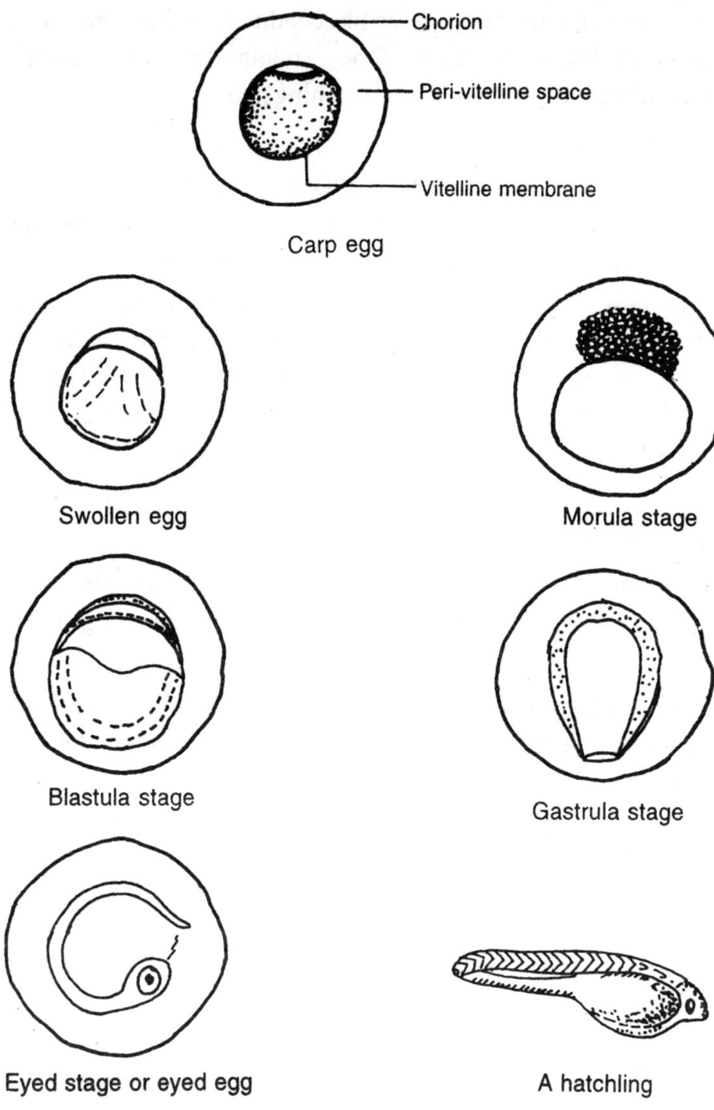

Fig. 7.5. Stages in the development of carp egg.

Size varies according to the seed production capacity of the hatchery. It is required for the continuous supply of uniformly cool water with sufficient pressure.

(b) Spawning pool or breeding pool

Spawning pool is a circular cement tank about 2 to 8 meters in diameter (size varies according to the requirements) and 1 to 1.5 meter deep. The bottom of the spawning pool slopes towards the centre into an outlet through a G.I. pipe leading to an incubator or hatching tank. The cemented wall of the spawning pool is provided with diagonally fitted inlet G.I. pipes for creating whirling movements in water. The periphery of the spawning tanks is provided with showers or small nozles for creating rainy season like conditions. After spawning and fertilization, the fertilized eggs accumulate at the centre of the spawning tank due to centrifugal force and pass through the GI outlet pipe in the incubator hatching pool.

Incubator or hatching pool

These are required for hatching of the fertilized eggs and also to ensure high survival by maintaining high concentration of dissolved oxygen. The incubator or hatching pool is a double chambered structure (Inner and outer circular cemented structure). The inner chamber in a hatching pool remain separataed from the outer chamber through a fine nylon screen (monofilament) fitted on a metal frame. Number and size of incubator or hatching pools varies according to the capacity of the hatchery. Generally, two hatching pools are connected with each breeding pool. Inside diameter of the hatching pool and egg holding capacity ranges from 70,000 to 1 million eggs cu. m^{-1} of pool. Diagonally fitted pipe with duck mouth opening are led to the bottom.

Spawn collection pool

These are subsurface rectangular cemented tanks of desirable size. The bottom of incubator outlet pipe opens into the spawn collection pool. The hatching spawn is collected in fine cloth.

Exercise 1 : Take out the gonads (male and female organs) from a catfish/carp during the different phases of reproductive cycle. Draw labelled diagrams and also plot GSI.

Exercise 2 : Fix the gonads (ovaries/testes), prepare histological slides and identify various stages

CHAPTER 8

Age, Growth and Population Studies

Experiment 8.1 **:** *To identify the type of scales.*

In fishes skin is generally covered with an exoskeleton in the form of scales. Catfishes have no scales. In living fishes scales are of several types viz. ganoid, placoid, cycloid and ctenoid scales.

(a) Placoid scales

Placoid scales has a disc like basal plate embedded in dermis and a trident spine projecting out through the epidermis. Outer covering of the spine is of enamel like hard transparent material called vitrodentine. Middle layer is dentine layer. Centre of the basal plate has an aperture. These scales occur in cartilaginous fishes such as sharks.

(b) Cycloid scales

Cycloid scales are also known as bony ridge scales, they are thin, flexible and transparent. They have characteristic ridges alternating with grooves. These ridges are like concentric rings. The central part is known as focus and is the first part to develop. They are present in the fishes belonging to order Cypriniformes.

(c) Ctenoid scales

Ctenoid scales have several spines on the surface of posterior area of the scale known as cteni. They are circular and have more or less serrated free edge. They are present in the fishes beloning to the order Perciformes.

For age determination, mostly scales, opercular bones, vertebrae and otoliths are used, however, fin ray's spines have also been tried in certain catfishes. Majority of the fresh water fishes have scales, hence, in Indian major carps, the use of scales for age determination have been fully authenticated. Fishes having deciduous scales e.g. *Cirrhinus reba* are not fit for age determination, hence, the alternate choice falls on either opercular bones or vertebrae.

Cycloid and ctenoid scales or their derivatives e.g. clupeoid or salmonid scales are used for age determination especially in regions which have distinct summer and winter season and the fishes have clear cut spawning periods. In India, age can be best determined in fishes inhabiting the waters of north India than South India.

Cosmoid, ganoid and placoid scales are not used for age determination. Cosmoid scales and ganoid scales occur only in primitive fishes e.g. *Latemeria* and *Lepidosteus*. Placoid scales are embedded in the skin of cartilaginous fishes. After attaining the maximum size, each placoid scale is shed off from the skin and new scale appears in place of old wornout scale.

Scale structure

The cycloid or ctenoid scales can be divided into anterior, posterior and lateral sides. In the centre, there is focus (may be absent in some fishes or old fishes), which may or may not be very distinct. Around the focus, growth lines in the form of circular lines or concentric rings called circuli are present. The circuli are clear in the posterior parts, where 2-3 circuli join to form one thick circuli.

Some distance from the focus, radii make their appearance at right angle to the circuli and cut the circuli. The anterior side of each scale is covered by the posterior part of the preceding scale. The posterior side of the scale is more thick, covered with epidermis and has colour pigments in the form of chromatophores. The structure or the cycloid and ctenoid scale is almost the same except that ctenoid scale has spines (cteni) on its posterior side, whereas, the cycloid scale has a smooth posterior side. The presence of cteni on the posterior side of the scale imparts roughness or sand paper like appearance to the fish's body surface.

Experiment 8.2 : *To determine the age of fish from hard parts.*

Age determination from scales

Materials

Forceps, scalpel, petridishes, binocular microscope, hand magnifying lens or scale reader.

Procedure

To determine the age of fish from scales, a sample should have the representative of all size groups. The scale should be collected from the left side of the fish, above the lateral line below the dorsal fin preferably from first or second row of the scales. The scale should be removed with the help of tweezers without damaging the scale (Fig. 8.1). Immediately after the removal, place the scales in an envelop in such a way that shining part of the scale should touch the paper. Record date and place of collection on the envelop. Total length, weight and sex of fish should also be recorded. Immediately after collection, place the scale containing envelop in sun-light to remove moisture and for the prevention of fungal attack.

At the time of observations, take out the scales from the envelops, wash them in tap water and rub between the finger tips to remove the dust particles, epidermis and other extraneous matter. Dry them and study under microfilm or scale reader..

Age determination (Fig. 8.2)

An annulus is formed on the scale periodically almost at the same time. In the annular zone several circuli show breaks and in some fishes this area appears to be a carved out space. The number of annuli present on the scale indicate the age (in years) of fish. A fish less than one

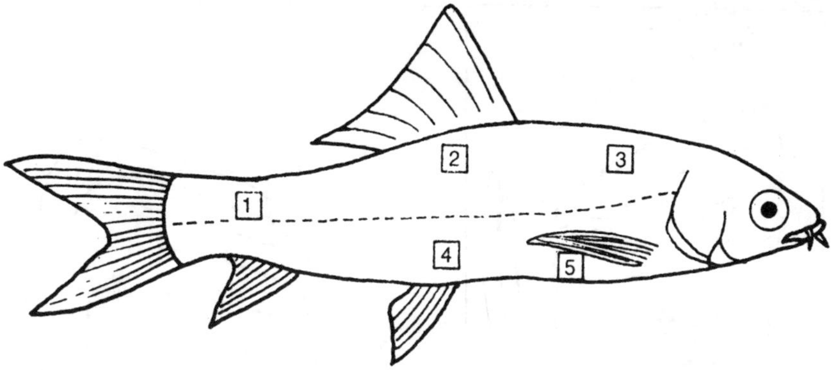

Fig. 8.1. Lateral side of fish body showing locations (1-5) from where the scales could be removed for age determination.

year will not have any annulus, but in some fishes very near to the focus there may be present larval mark, sometimes one can confuse with the first year mark. A fish less than one year is said to belong to 'O' age class, with 1,2,3,4,5 annuli to age classes 1,2,3,4 and 5 respectively.

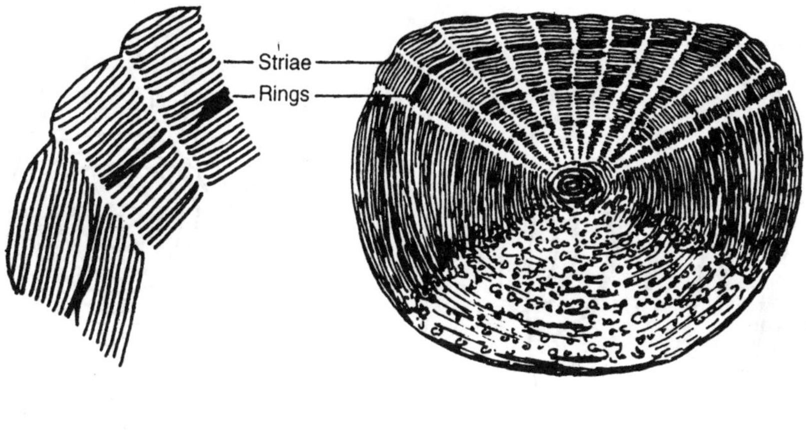

Fig. 8.2. Scale of *Tilapia galidaea* with annual marks.

Opercular bones and vertebrae

Left opercular bone and 9th, 10th, 11th or 12th vertebrae are commonly employed for age determination. To collect these two hard parts, the fish has to be sacrified. Remove the opercular bone and the desired vertebrae and keep these structures in water for 20 minutes at 60°C. Thereafter, remove the muscles with soft tooth-brush, clear in tap water, give a dip in 50% hydrogen peroxide for 30 minutes and sun-dry for 24 h. Preserve the bones in envelops for 2-3 months. Annuli will become clear with the passage of time. Count the number of annuli, which will indicate the age in years (Fig. 8.3 and 8.4).

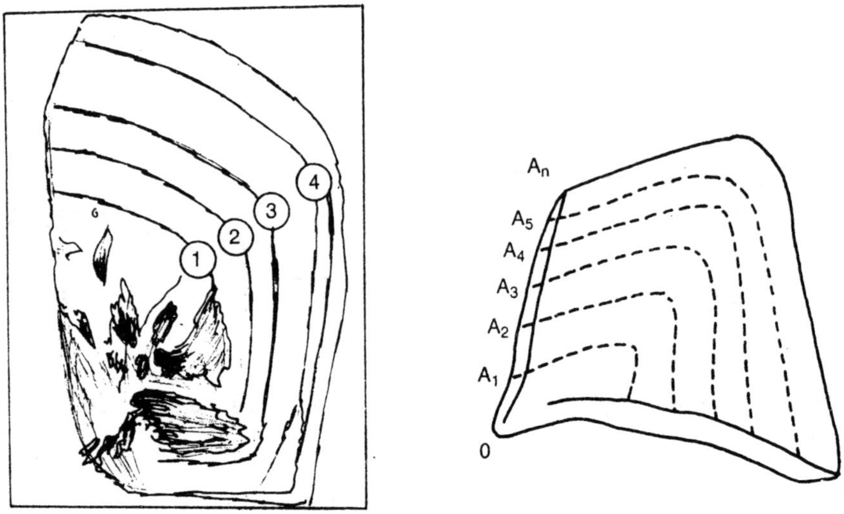

(a) (b)

Fig. 8.3. (a) Opercular bone of *Labeo calbasu*—age 4 years. (b) Mode of measurement of opercular bone.

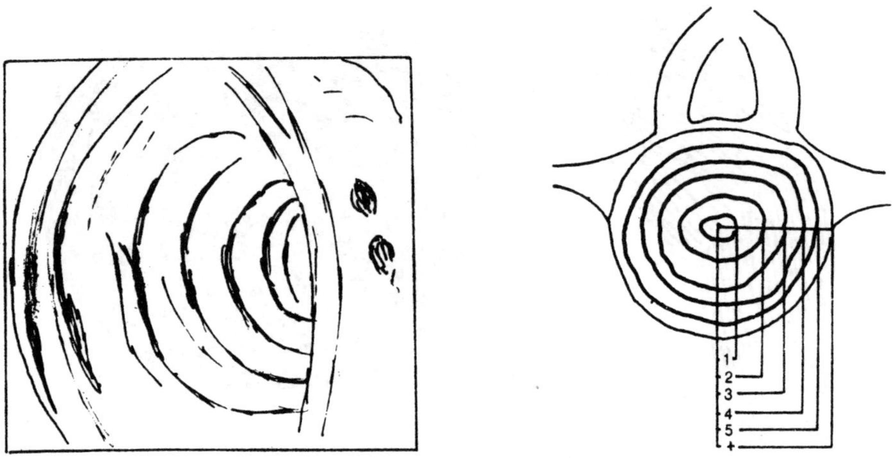

(a) (b)

Fig. 8.4. (a) Vertebra of *Tor putitora*—age 7 years. (b) Mode of measurement of vertebra.

Otoliths

By giving a cut on the dorsal side of the auditory capsule, remove the sagitta. If the sagitta is transparent, preserve it in cedar wood oil for 1 to 2 months and the rings will become clear. Study the otolith by placing it in the cavity slide. Count the rings. If the otolith is translucent or the rings are not clear,then fix the otolith in arldite and grind it on the corundum stone, initially on the rough grain and finally on the fine grain. Then polish it by grinding it on the fine sand paper coated with wax. Rings will become clear. Study as such under the binocular microscope. The number of rings will indicate the age in years (Fig. 8.5).

Length 67 cm Age 3 years

Magnification × 16

Fig. 8.5. Otolith of a cod—age 3 years.

Experiment 8.3 : *To find out the growth pattern of fish by determining length-weight relationship.*

Principle

Weight in fishes may be considered as a function of length. An ideal fish follow the cube law according to which the weight of fish equals the cube of length times a constant.

$$W = cL^n$$

Where,

W = weight

L = length

c = constant

n = exponent

Materials

(i) Measuring scale

(ii) Weighing balance

Procedure

- Collect the specimens of the experimental fish and arrange them in the ascending order keeping in mind the size.
- Measure the total length (in cm, length from snout to the end of caudal fin) and note the weight in grams.
- Tabulate the data as given in the table 18.
- Multiply log L and log W for each of paired values.
- Note down the number of paired observations.
- Calculate 'c' and 'n' according to the formula given below.
- Also calculate coefficient of correlation 'r' for length and weight.

Table 18. Observations

S.No.	Length (cm)	Weight (g)	Log L (L)	Log W (w)	Log L × Log W

Calculations

Σ log L (ΣX) | Σ log W (ΣY) | Σ log L × log W (ΣXY)

Σ log L^2 (ΣX^2) | Σ log W^2 (ΣY^2)

Mean log L ($\bar{X}$) | Mean log W ($\bar{Y}$)

Calculate sum of squares as follows

$$xy = \Sigma XY - \frac{(\Sigma X) \times (\Sigma Y)}{N}$$

$$x^2 = \Sigma X^2 - \frac{(\Sigma X)^2}{N}$$

$$y^2 = \Sigma Y^2 - \frac{(\Sigma Y)^2}{N}$$

$$b = \frac{xy}{x^2} \qquad b = n$$

$$a = \bar{Y} - b\bar{X} \qquad a = c$$

N = number of fishes examined

$$W = cL^n$$

$$\text{Coefficient of correlation (r)} = \frac{\sigma xy}{\sqrt{\sigma x^2 \times \sigma y^2}}$$

Experiment 8.4 : *To determine the condition factor or index of condition of given fish.*

Theory

The condition factor of a fish indicate the well being of the fish in a particular environment.

It also reflects the feeding condition in the environment. Condition factor (cf) can be numerically determined for the given species of fish, in the given environment using the formula given below.

Procedure

- Collect the specimens randomly and measure their length and coresponding weights covering all seasons.
- Calculate condition factor (cf) separately for different seasons, as the condition of a species varies with seasons.

Calculation

$$cf = \frac{\text{Weight} \times 10^5}{L^3}$$

(Weight may be given in g and length in mm)

Experiment 8.5 : *To calculate the population of a fish pond by Peterson's method, taking glass beads as fish.*

Materials

(i) Bowl

(ii) Beads of different colours

(iii) $KMnO_4$ crystals

Principle

This method of determining fish population depends on the recovery of marked or tagged fishes.

Procedure

- Fill the bowl half with water.
- Put some $KMnO_4$ crystals so that the bottom becomes invisible.
- Add counted number of glass beads and spread them uniformly.
- Take out some beads by hand. Count and replace these with coloured beads.
- Repeat the process till 20% of the population becomes marked or tagged.
- Count the marked and unmarked beads (fish) captured in each trial. Repeat the trial atleast ten times and make a table (Table 19).

Calculations

Calculate the population of fishes of a water body using following formula :

$$P = \frac{\Sigma(m)\ (u+r)}{\Sigma\ r}$$

Where,

m = Total number of marked fish

u = Total number of unmarked fish

r = Total No. of marked fish recaptured

.also calculate % error by determining actual population and calculated population.

Table 19.

Observation record

	Unmarked fish captured (u)	Marked fishes capured (r)
1		
2		
3		
4		
5		
6		
7		
8		
9		
10		
	Σ(u) =	Σ (r) =

Experiment 8.6 : *Calculate the total population of fish in a pond by Delury's method taking glass beads as fishes.*

Materials

(i) Bowl

(ii) Glass beads

(iii0 $KMnO_4$ crystals

Procedure

Put some water in the bowl and a very few crystals of $KMnO_4$, so that the water becomes red and bottom becomes invisible. Now add counted number of beads, shake them. Put the hand inside and take out some beads from one place without lifting the hand. Count the number of beads. Again, shake the solution and take out more beads. Repeat the same effort about 10 times and count the total number of beads taken out. Make the record and calculate the accumulated catch.

Suppose

No. of trials = 12

Total beads taken out = 382

Cumulative catch = 2657

The equation to be used for calculation are :

$$\Sigma(y) = a + b\,\Sigma(x) \quad \ldots(1)$$

$$\Sigma(xy) = a\Sigma(x) + b\Sigma(x)^2 \quad \ldots(2)$$

$$y = a + b.x \quad \ldots(3)$$

Where,

a = y = intercept

b = slope of line

N = No. of trials = 12

Σx = Kt = 2657

Σy = ct = 382

$x_1y_1 = 0\times39 = 0$

$x_2y_2 = 70\times32 = 2240$

$x_3y_3 = 103\times42 = 4326$

$x_4y_4 = 145\times34 = 5930$

$x_5y_5 = 179\times39 = 6265$

$x_6y_6 = 214\times42 = 8988$

$x_7y_7 = 256\times26 = 6656$

$x_8y_8 = 282\times28 = 7896$

$x_9y_9 = 310\times28 = 8680$

$x_{10}y_{10} = 338\times28 = 9464$

$x_{11}y_{11} = 366\times28 = 10248$

$x_{12}y_{12} = 394\times20 = 7880$

$\Sigma(xy) = 78573$

Again

$$\Sigma(x)^2 = X^2_1 + x_2^2 + x^2_3 + x_4^2 + ...$$

$$x^2_1 = 0^2 = 0$$

$$x^2_2 = (70)^2 = 4900$$

$$x^2_3 = (103)^2 = 10609$$

$$x^2_4 = (145)^2 = 21025$$

$$x^2_5 = (179)^2 = 32041$$

$$x^2_6 = (214)^2 = 45796$$

$$x^2_7 = (256)^2 = 65536$$

$$x^2_8 = (282)^2 = 79524$$

$$x^2_9 = (310)^2 = 96100$$

$$x^2_{10} = (338)^2 = 114244$$

$$x^2_{11} = (366)^2 = 133956$$

$$x^2_{12} = (394)^2 = 155236$$

$$\Sigma(xy)^2 = 758967$$

Putting these values in equation

$$\Sigma(y) = \sqrt{a} + b\,\Sigma(x)$$

$$382 = 12a + 2657b$$

$$12a = 382\text{-}2657b$$

$$a = \frac{382\text{-}2657b}{12} \quad ...(4)$$

Putting the value of 'a' in equation (2)

$$\Sigma(xy) = a\,\Sigma(x) + b\Sigma\,(x^2)$$

$$78573 = \frac{382\text{-}2657b}{12} \times 2657 + b \times 758967$$

$$78573 = \frac{1014974 - 7059649\,b}{12} + 758967\,b$$

$$= \frac{1014974\text{-}7059649b + 9107604b}{12}$$

$$78573 = \frac{1014974 - 2047955\ b}{12}$$

$$942876\text{-}1014974 = 2047955b$$

$$\frac{-72098}{2047955} = b$$

$$b = -0.0352$$

Substituting the value of 'b' in 4.

$$a = \frac{382\text{-}2657 \times (-0.0350)}{12} \quad \ldots(4)$$

$$a = 39.5829$$

Now putting the values of 'a' and 'b' in equation (3), and taking the arbitrary values for 'x' [y = (a+b x)]

$x_1 = 10$ $y_1 = 39.58 - 0.35 = 39.23$
$x_2 = 20$ $y_2 = 39.58 - 0.70 = 38.88$
$x_3 = 30$ $y_3 = 39.58 - 1.05 = 38.53$
$x_4 = 40$ $y_4 = 39.58 - 1.40 = 37.13$
$x_5 = 50$ $y_5 = 39.58 - 1.75 = 37.83$
$x_6 = 60$ $y_6 = 39.58 - 2.10 = 37.48$
$x_7 = 70$ $y_7 = 39.58 - 2.45 = 37.13$
$x_8 = 80$ $y_8 = 39.58 - 2.80 = 36.78$
$x_9 = 90$ $y_9 = 39.58 - 3.15 = 36.43$
$x_{10} = 100$ $y_{10} = 39.58 - 3.50 = 36.08$

now, by putting these values of 'x' and 'y' on graph the total population =

Percentage error

Total actual population = $= \alpha$

Calculated population = $= \beta$

$$\text{Percentage error} = \frac{(\alpha - \beta)}{\alpha} \times 100$$

Exercise 1. Collect scales from different fish species and use for determining the age of the species

Exercise 2: On the basis of the given length-size data, draw histograms of appropriate size groups and give suitable interpretation of the data

Sr.No.	Months					
	May		August		November	
	Size (cm)	No. of fishes	Size (cm)	No. of fishes	Size (cm)	No. of fishes
1.	10.5	12	14.2	22	14.7	80
2.	10.7	20	14.0	300	15.3	25
3.	10.2	17	14.1	200	2.3	300
4.	10.3	7	14.3	125	2.1	200
5.	10.6	11	15.2	17	2.9	17
6.	10.8	9	!5.4	12	2.0	15
7.	10.1	0	15.3	9	2.2	125
8.	12.5	3	15.0	7	2.4	10
9.	12.6	37	15.1	10	2.6	20
10.	12.8	75	10.2	75	3.1	10
11.	12.9	25	12.5	37	3.0	5
12.	12.7	5			2.8	5
13.					3.1	7
14.					2.7	9
15.					2.5	2

Calculation

Size group for the landing of May month

I	10.1 - 10.5	12+7+17	= 36
II	10.6 - 11.0	11+9+20	= 40
III	12.1 - 12.5	3	= 3
IV	12.6 - 13.0	37+5+25+75	= 142
		G. Total	221

Size group and their landing in August

I	10.1 - 10.5	75	= 75
II	12.1 - 12.5	37	= 37
III	13.6 - 14.0	300	= 300
IV	14.1 - 14.5	200+22+125	= 347
V	14.6 - 15.0	7	= 7
VI	15.1 - 15.5	10+17+12+9	= 48
		G. Total	814

Size group of November and total landing

I	2.0 - 2.5	300+200+125+10+15+2	= 652
II	2.6 - 3.0	9+5+20+17+5	= 56
III	3.1 - 3.5	10+7	= 17
IV	3.6 - 4.0	0	= 0
V	14.6 - 15.0	80	= 80
VI	15.1 - 15.5	25	= 25
		G. Total	830

Results

On the basis of data given above we can say that in the month of May the most abundant size was 12.6 to 13.0 cm (142 fishes i.e. 64.5% of total catch). In the month of August the size group ranging between 14.1 to 14.5 was the highest (i.e. 79.4% of total catch). In the month of November 652 fishes were in the size group of 2.0-2.5 cm and ranked Ist i.e. 78.5% of the total catch. We can say from these results that the most younger stage are found after spawning season is over and thus the spawning period of the fish is around August.

Exercise 3 : *Plot a graph between anterior scale radius and mean total length of a fish from the following data :*

Anterior scale radius (mm)	Mean total length (mm)
9.5	26.6
12.7	33.0
22.4	43.1
35.6	55.5
44.9	65.2
55.5	74.2
65.3	84.1
78.3	94.7
98.6	104.7
106.3	124.0
116.7	133.4
138.3	154.0
152.2	175.0
178.0	194.6
183.3	203.1
190.5	214.3
200.1	230.4
210.0	234.4
222.4	243.4
226.0	252.0
232.9	235.0

Exercise 4 . What is CF and explain the following formula :

$$L' = \frac{S'}{S}(L-CF) + CF$$

Ans. The meaning of the parts of the above formula are as follows :

CF = Correction factor (constant)

L' = Length of the fish at any annulus 'n'

L = Length of the fish at the time of caputre

S' = Anterior scale radius to annulus 'n'

S = Anterior scale radius that is distance from focus to margin of the scale

Correction Factor (C.F.) is a constant length of the fish at the time of the scale formation and can be accurately determined using correction factor.

Calculate the scale radius measurements for the following data :

where

(i)	CF	= 10 mm
(ii)	Scale marginal radius in mm at the time of exploitation	= 130
(iii)	Length of the fish at the time of capture/ standard length in mm	= 280
(iv)	Computed length/length of the fish annulus 'n' L_1	= (a) 80 (b) 160 (c) 190 (d) 230 (e) 350

S = 130 mm

S' = ?

L = 280

L'_a = 80

L'_b = 160

L'_c = 190

L_d' = 230

L'_e = 350

Formulae

$$L' = \frac{S'}{S}(L-CF) + CF$$

$$S' = \frac{S(L'-CF)}{(L-CF)}$$

$$S' = \frac{130(80-10)}{(280-10)}$$

(a) $$S' = \frac{130(70)}{(270)} = \frac{9100}{270} = 33.7 \text{ mm}$$

(b) $$S' = \frac{130(160-10)}{(280-10)} = 72.22 \text{ mm}$$

(c) $S' = \dfrac{130(190-10)}{(280-10)} = 86.66$ mm

(d) $S' = \dfrac{130(230-10)}{(280-10)} = 105.92$ mm

(e) $S' = \dfrac{130(350-10)}{(280-10)} = 163.70$ mm

Exercise 5. Compute the standard length for the following data where (a) the scale marginal radius at the time of capture was 120 mm, (b) Standard length 250 mm, (c) anterior scale radius measurements 30.0, 70.0, 90.0, 100.0, 110.0mm.

Ans. By using unmodified formula :

(i) $L' = L \dfrac{S'}{S}$

Where

S = 120 mm

$S'_a = 30.0$ $S'_b = 70.0$ $S'_c = 90.0$ $S'_d = 100.0$ $S'_e = 110.0$

$L = 250$ $L' = ?$

$$L' = L \frac{S'}{S}$$

(a) $L' = \dfrac{250 \times 30.0}{120} = 62.5$

(b) $L' = \dfrac{250 \times 70.0}{120} = 145.83$

(c) $L' = \dfrac{250 \times 90.0}{120} = 187.5$

(d) $L' = \dfrac{250 \times 100.0}{120} = 208.33$

(e) $L' = \dfrac{250 \times 110.0}{120} = 229.16$

(ii) If correction Factor is 10 (CF = 10), apply modified formula :

$$L' = \frac{S'}{S}(L\text{-}CF)+CF$$

(a) $L' = \dfrac{30.0}{120}(250-10) + 10 = 70$

(b) $L' = \dfrac{70.0}{120}(240) + 10 = 150$

(c) $L' = \dfrac{90.0}{120}(240) + 10 = 190$

(d) $L' = \dfrac{100.0}{120}(240) + 10 = 210$

(e) $L' = \dfrac{110.0}{120}(240) + 10 = 230$

(iii) Plot the data of the results obtained and find out the nature of relationship

Ans.

	S' data (mm)	L' results (mm)
(a)	30.0	62.5
(b)	70.0	145.83
(c)	90.0	187.5
(d)	100.0	208.33
(e)	110.0	229.16

Exercise 6 . Calculate length and weigth relationship from the following data given for a fish population.

Total length in centimeters	Average weight in kg
10.5	1.00
12.0	1.39
14.0	2.47
15.0	3.17
16.0	3.93
18.0	4.54
19.0	6.14
20.0	6.80
21.0	7.00
22.0	10.65

Plot average weight in kg against total length in centimeters. It merely show you the form of length weight relationship. Take common logarithms of the above two columns of data, i.e. total length in centimeters and average weight in kg. Plot log weight against log length on a graph paper. Draw a straight line.

Exercise 7 : If total population = 1000, unmarked population= 900, marked population = 100, calculate population of fish and per cent error

Unmarked fish captured (u)	Marked fish captured (r)
50	9
32	4
20	0
20	1
13	2
10	3
12	0
10	1
8	1
6	0
Σ (u) = 181	Σ(r) = 21

m = marked population = 100

$$P = \frac{\Sigma(m)\ (u+r)}{(r)}$$

$$P = \frac{100\,(181+21)}{(21)}$$

$$P = \frac{100 \times 202}{(21)} = 961$$

To get % age error

Actual population = 1000

Calculated population = 961

$$\%\ \text{age error} = \frac{39 \times 100}{1000}$$

Ans. 3.9%

CHAPTER 9

Key for the Identification of Common Fishes

1. Anal fin confluent with caudal; jaws toothed; head with muciferous channels .... Order : Osteoglossiformes
Suborder : Notopteroidei
Family : Notopteridae
Genus : *Notopterus*

Cleft of mouth extends opposite middle of the orbit; body without hump; caudal without spots .... *N. notopterus* (Pallas)

Cleft of mouth extends far beyond the orbit; body with distinct hump; caudal peduncle with black spots .... *N. chitala* (Ham.)

2. Body covered with cycloid scales; barbels if present small; adipose fin absent .... Order : Cypriniformes
Suborder : Cyprinoidei 4

Body naked; barbels long especially maxillary; adipose fin present or absent .... Order : Siluriformes
Suborder : Siluroidei 18

Jaws not produced into beak 3

3. Head covered with large plate-like scales; ventral fins spineless .... Order : Channiformes
Family : Channidae
Genus : *Channa*
(Syn. Ophiocephalus

(i) Anal rays 20-30 i

Anal rays 25-35 iii

(ii) Lateral line scales 37-40, lateral line with slight break between 13th and 15th scale; dorsal fin rays 29-30. .... *C. punctatus* (Bloch)

Lateral line scales 40-45, lateral line descends after 12th scale; dorsal fin rays 32-37; young specimens with a spot on last rays .... *C. gachua* (Ham.)

(iii) Anal rays 25-27; dorsal fin rays 37-45; lateral line scales 57-60, lateral line descends below 12th dorsal ray .... *C. striatus* (Bloch)

Anal rays 30-35; dorsal rays 53-55; lateral line scales 60-70, lateral line descends after 16th to 18th scale; a black white edged ocellus on tail .... *C. marulius* (Ham.)

Head without scales; ventral fins with one spine and five rays or each ventral reduced to single filamentous ray or ventral fins united to form a sucking disc .... Order : Perciformes 27

4. Eyes prominent; barbels four or less; suborbital spines absent .... Family : Cyprinidae 5

5. Abdomen rounded 6

6. Lateral line close to the middle of body .... Sub-family : Cyprininae 7

7. Dorsal fin commencing in advance of ventrals; anal with 5-8 rays 8

8. Mouth upturned .... Genus : *Catla*
C. catla (Ham.)

Mouth not upturned 9

9. Mouth inferior 10

Mouth terminal 14

10. Adhesive disc absent on the lower lip 11

11. Lip (s) thick, continuous at the angles of mouth 12

Lip (s) thin, not continuous at the angles of mouth 13

12. Only upper lip thick fleshy; mandible neither broad, flattened nor with a sharp margin, its edge sometimes with deciduous horny covering; barbels 4(2 rostral and 2 maxillary) .... Genus : *Schizothorax*
Schizothorax sp.

One or both lips possessing soft and moveable horny coverings; barbels 4 or 2, if two maxillary .... Genus : *Labeo*

(i) With four barbels ii

With two barbels v

(ii) Dorsal rays 16-19 iii

(iii) Ll. 74-84 .... *L. gonius* (Ham.)

Ll. 40-45 .... *L. calbasu* (Ham.)

(iv) Tubercles on the symphysis of lower jaw, no horny covering on jaws; black spot on 5th-6th lateral line scale .... *L. bata* (Ham.)

(v) Dorsal rays 15-16 .... *L. rohita* (Ham.)

13. No callous pad on the under surface of lower jaw .... Genus : *Cirrhinus*

Dorsal rays 10-11 .... *C. reba* (Ham.)

Dorsal rays 13-16 .... *C. mrigala* (Ham.)

14. Dorsal fin short with not more than eleven rays; barbels 4, 2 or none .... Genus : *Puntius*

(i) Barbels present ii

Barbels absent ix

(ii) With two barbels iii

With four barbels v

(iii) Last undivided dorsal ray osseous and entire; lateral line with 25-26 lateral line scales iv

Last undivided dorsal ray osseous and entire; lateral line with 26-28 lateral line scales; one band of spots in upper half and another at the base of the dorsal fin .... *P. chola* (Ham.)

(iv) Dark lateral blotch on 22-24 lateral line scales; one oblique band in the centre of dorsal fin, black spot behind gill opening .... *P. tetrarupagus* (McClelland)

(v) Last undivided dorsal ray osseous and serrated vi

(vi) Lateral line scales 32-34 .... *P. sarana* (Ham.)

Lateral line scales 24 .... *P. sarana subnaustus* (Cuv. & Val.)

(vii) Last undivided dorsal ray osseous and serrated viii

(viii) Lateral line complete ix

(ix) Lateral line scales 23-24; two black spots, first on 3rd and 4th and second on 20-21 lateral line scales .... *P. punctatus* Day

Lateral line ceases before 12th scale x

(x) Lateral line ceases after 6th to 8th scale; black spot on 15th-17th lateral line scales and another at commencement of lateral line ...... *P. ticto* (Ham.)

(xi) Lateral line scales 23-26; black spot on 22nd and 23rd lateral line scales and another on 3rd-5th divided dorsal ray .... *P. stigma* (Day)

Dorsal fin long with 17-23 rays 15

15. Barbels four .... Genus : *Cyprinus*

LI . scales 28; scales large and irregular in size .... *C. carpio* var. specularis (Linn.)

LI. scales 38; scales small and of equal size .... *C. carpio* var. *communis* (Linn.)

Barbels absent .... Genus : *Carassius*

C. carassius (Linn.)

16. Lateral line with irregular course; anal with 14-15 rays ....Genus : *Hypophthalmichthys*

H. molitrix (Cuv. and Val.)

17. Anal rays 13-14; cleft of mouth directed somewhat upward, lower jaw prominent with knob above the symphysis; lateral line concave in two parts .... Genus : *Chela*

(Syn. *Oxygaster*)

(i) Lateral line scales 32-33; anal rays 24...... *C. labuca* (Ham.)

Lateral line scales 80-160; anal rays 13-21 ii

(ii) Lateral line scales 80-110 iii

(iii) Anal rays 13-15 .... *C. bacaila* (Ham.)

18. Dorsal fin spineless; adipose dorsal absent 27

19. Anal fin long (31-73 rays) .... Family : Schilbeidae .. 26

20. Nostrils far apart, posterior with a nasal barbel. Family : Bagridae ... 22

21. Gill openings narrow 24

22. Barbels six; each ventral fin with eight rays; cubito-humeral process present .... Genus : *Rita*

R. rita (Ham.)

Barbels eight; each ventral fin with six rays 23

23. Eyes prominent with free circular margin; dorsal and pectoral spines not very strong; head generally with median longitudinal groove .... Genus : *Mystus*

(i) Median longitudinal groove on the head reaches the base of the occipital process ii

Median longitudinal groove on the head does not reach the base of the occipital process vi

(ii) Maxillary barbels reach the anal fin or even extend to caudal iii

Maxillary barbels do not reach the anal fin v

(iii) Black spot present on the adipose dorsal fin; interneural shield present; adipose fin less than the length of the base of the dorsal fin .... *M. aor* (Ham.)

Black spot present on the adipose dorsal fin; interneural shield absent iv

(iv) Maxillary barbels reach the anal fin; adipose dorsal commences just behind the rayed dorsal fin and extends beyond anal .... *M. bleekeri* (Day)

Maxillary barbels reach the base of the caudal fin; adipose fin long, commencing just behind the last ray of rayed dorsal fin .... *M. cavasius* (Ham.)

(v) Interneural shield present between the occipital process and basal bone of dorsal; maxillary barbels reach the hind edge of the first dorsal fin; black spot present at the posterior side of lthe adipose dorsal fin .... *M. seenghala* (Sykes)

Interneural shield absent; maxillary barbels reach the base of the ventrals; adipose dorsal fin starts from the base of the last undivided dorsal ray and 1/3 of the total length of rayed dorsal fin .... *M. tengara* (Ham.)

(vi) Maxillary barbels reach beyond the base of the ventrals or little beyond them or upto anal; length of the adipose fin equals that of the base of rayed dorsal fin plus the intermediate space; granules on the head do not form lines; longitudinal groove narrow, tapering abruptly to a point .... *M. vittatus* (Bloch)

24. Dorsal fin absent; anal rays 71-73 .... Genus : *Ailia A. coila* (Ham.)

25. Dorsal fin short with 4-5 rays; barbels four; accessory respiratory organs absent .... Family : Siluridae 26

Dorsal fin with more than six rays; barbels eight; accessory respiratory organs prersent 27

26. Cleft of mouth ends behind eyes; anal rays rays 84-96 ....Genus : *Wallago*

W. attu (Bl. & Schn.)

Cleft of mouth ends in front of eyes; anal rays 54-75 .... Genus : *Callichrous* (Syn.Ompok)

(i) Maxillary barbels reach the end of the pectoral fin; pectoral spine feebly serrated; anal rays 54-60 .... *C. pabda* (Ham.)

Maxillary barbels reach the ventral fins or the middle of the body; pectoral spine strongly or moderately serrated ii

(ii) Maxillary barbels reach the ventral fins; pectoral fin reaches the anal fin; anal rays 54-57 .... *C. bimaculatus* (Bloch)

Maxillary barbels reach the middle of the body; pectoral fins reach 4th or 5th anal ray; anal rays 69-73 .... *C. macrophthalmus* (Blyth)

27. Dorsal fin with 62-76 rays; anal rays 45-58 .... Family: *Clariidae*

Genus: *Clarias*

C. batrachus (Linn.)

Dorsal fin with 6-7 rays; anal rays 60-79 .... Family : *Heteropneustidae*

Genus: *Heteropneustes* (Syn.Saccobranchus)

H. fossilis (Bloch)

S. fossilis (Bloch)

28. Ventral fins moderately apart 29

29. Each ventral fin with one spine and five rays .... Suborder: Percoidei 30

Each ventral fin reduced to single filamentous ray .... Suborder: Anabantoidei

Family: *Anabantidae*
Genus: *Trichogaster*

(Syn. *Colisa*).

D.xv-xvii/9-15; A.xvi/xviii/16-18; pyloric caecae present .... *T. fasciatus* (Bl. & Schn.)

D. xv-xvi/7-8; A.xvii-xviii/13-15; pyloric caecae absent .... *T. lailus* Ham.)

30. Anal rays 11-12; lateral line interrupted at 32nd or 40th scale, restarting after leaving three rows of scales below, continuing upto base of caudal fin .... Family: Nandidae

Genus; *Nandus*

N. nandus (Ham.)

Anal rays 16-20; lateral line complete or indistinct .... Family: Ambassidae
(Syn. Centropomidae
Genus: *Ambassis*
(Syn. *Chanda*)

(i) Lateral line indistinct; canines present ....*A. nama* (Ham.)

Lateral line distinct; canines absent .... **ii**

(ii) Lateral line with 60-62 scales ....*A. ranga* (Ham.)

Lateral line with 80 scales .... *A. baculis* (Ham.)

31. Mouth somewhat superior, cleft of mouth oblique, extending below anterior margin of orbit; canines absent; caudal obtuse; lateral line absent .... Genus : *Glossogobius*
(Syn. *Gobius* (Ham.)
G. giuris
(Syn. *G. gutum* (Ham.)

Mouth superior, cleft of mouth oblique extending below anterior half of orbit, recurved teeth on jaws, canines present; caudal rounded .... Genus ; *Acentrogobius*
A. viridipunctatus
(Cuv. and Val.)

FISH IDENTIFICATION CHART

I. Name of fish

II. Morphometric relationship (Fig. 9.1)

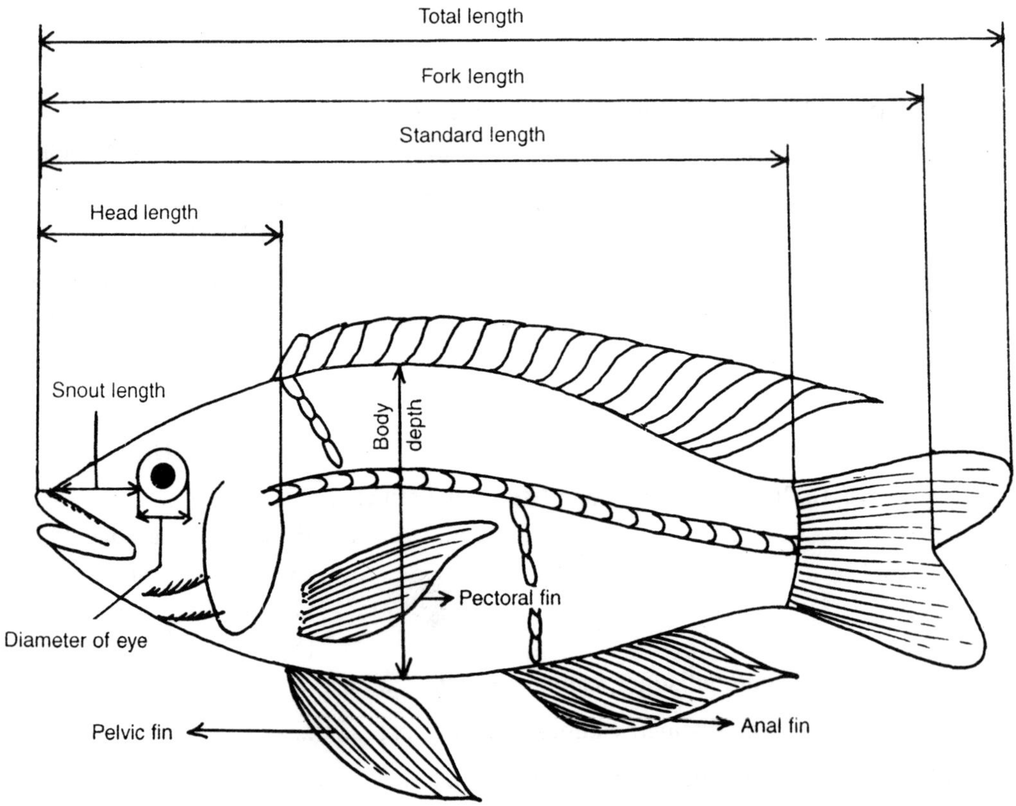

Fig. 9.1. Figure showing how morphometric measurements are made.

Sr. No.	Character	Measurement
1.	Total length	
2.	Standard length	
3.	Length of Head	
4.	Snout length	
5.	Diameter of eye	
6.	Height of body	
7.	Body girth	
8.	Caudal peduncle	

III. Fin formula

Dorsal	Pectoral	Ventral	Anal	Caudal

IV. Scale count

(a) Lateral line scale

(b) Scales above lateral line

(c) Scales below lateral line

V. Other characters

VI. Habit and Habitat

VII. Systematic position

Exercise 1 : Collect the common fish fauna from ponds/tanks and canals, identify, classify and write characters.

Bibliography

AOAC (Association of Official Analytical Chemists) 1995. Official methods of analysis. Assoc. Of Anal. Chem. Washington, DC, USA.

APHA (American Public Health Assocation) 1998. Standard methods for the examination of water and waste water, 20th edn. APHA, AWWA, WPFC, Washington, DC.

Das, R.K. 1997. Microbial indices for assessing aquatic productivity. Summer school on fisheries enhancement in small reservoirs and flood plain lakes CIFRI Barrackpore, **4** : 37-41.

Henken, A.M., Lucas, H., Tijssen, P.A.T. and Machiels, M.A.M. 1986. A comparison between methods used to determine the energy content of feed, fish and faeces samples. Aquaculture, **58** : 195-201.

Houssay, B.A. 1931. Action sexualle de l'hypophyse surles poisons et les reptiles. C.R. Soc. Biol. **106** : 377-378.

Margalef, R. 1958. Information theory in ecology. Gen. Syst. **3** : 36-71.

Shannon, C.E. and Weaver, W. 1963. The mathematical theory of communication. University of Illinois Press, Urbana, Il.

Snell, F.D. 1978. Photometric and fluorometric methods of analysis : Metals (Part 2). John Wiley and Sons, Inc., New York.

Washington, H.G. 1984. Diversity, biotic and similarity indices. Water Res. **18**(6) : 653-694.

List of Abbreviations

@	at the rate of	d	day
BW	body weight	mci	microcurie
cm	centimetre	nm	namometer
cu.mm	cubic millimetre	wks	weeks
g	gram	a	alpha
ha	hectare	b	beta
h	hour (in cone sampler h = height)	ppt	parts per thousand
kg	kilogram	ppm	parts per million
l, L	litre	mm	micrometre
mm	millimetre	°C	degree Celsius
ml	millilitre	ml	microlitre
mg	milligram	min	minutes
m	metre	rpm	revolutions per minute
No.	number	wt	weight
W	week	w/v	weight by volume (2 g of NaOH per 100 ml of water)
Y	year		
mS^{-1}	metre per second	v/v	volume by volume (2 ml of HCl per 100 ml of water)
S	sigma		
N	normal	w/w	weight by weight (2 g of HCl per 100 g of water)

Suggested Readings

Agarwal, S.C. and Johal, M.S. 1998. Fishery Development. Narendra Publishing House, Delhi.

Bagenal,T. 1978. Methods for assessment of fish production in fresh waters, IBP Handbook No. 3 Blackwell Scientific Publications, Oxford.

Bardach, J.E. Ryther, J.H. and Mclarnely, O.W. 1972. Aquaculture. Wiley Interscience.

Benjamin, M.M. 1978. Outline of veterinary clinical pathology. The Iowa State University Press Iowa USA, 3rd edition.

Blom, J.H. 1988. Chemical and physical water quality analysis. A report on practical training at the faculty of fisheries. Brawijaya University, Malang Indonesia.

Boyd, C.E. 1982. Water quality management for pond fish culture. Developments in Aquaculture and Fisheries Science. I. Elsevier Scientific Publishing Company, Amsterdam.

Davy, B. and Graham, M. (eds.) 1979. Diseases of fish cultured for food in south east Asia : report of a workshop held in cisarua, Bagor, Indonesia,International Development Research Centre, Otawa, Canada.

Delince, G. 1992. The ecology of the fish pond ecosystem. Kluwer Academic Publishers, Netherlands, 230 pp.

Golterman, H.L., Clymo, R.S. and M.A.M. Ohnstad, 1978. Methods for physical and chemical analysis of fresh waters. Blackwell Scientific Publications, Oxford, 213 pp.

Hepher, B. 1975. Supplementary feeding in fish culture. In Nutrition and production of fish. Vol. 3. S. Karger, Basel, pp. 183-198.

Hoar, W.S., Randall, D.J. and Donaldson, E. M. 1983. Fish physiology. Volume IXA and IXB. Reproduction. Academic Press, London.

Huet, M. 1972. Text book of fish culture-breeding and cultivation of fish, England : Fishing News (Books) Ltd.

Jhingran, V.G. 1983. Fish and fisheries of India. Hindustan Publishing Corporation (India) pp. 954.

Jhingran, V.G. and Pullin, R.S.V. 1988. A hatchery manual for the common, chinese and Indian major carps. Asian development bank. ICLARM, Philippines, pp. 163.

Needham, J.G. and P.R. Needham, 1962. A guide to the study of fresh water biology. Holden Berg, San Francisco, USA, 107pp.

Piper, C.S. 1950. Soil and plant analysis. University of Adelaide, Australia.

Pillai, T.V.R. and Dill, W.M.A. (Eds.) 1979. Advances in Aquaculture, England : fishing News (Books) Ltd. England.

Roberts, R.J. (editor) 1978. Fish pathology. Bailliere Tindall, London, pp. 318.

Roberts, R.J. 1978. Miscellaneous non-infection diseases. In R.J. Roberts (ed.) Fish pathology Baillere Tindall, London, 227-234 pp.

Schowerbel, J. 1970. Methods of hydrobiology. Pergamon Press Oxford.

Wetzel, R.G. and Likens, G.E. 1979. Limnological analysis, W.B. Saunders Co. Philadelphia, London, Toronto.